To: Tiffany
7/29/17

AF807860

Moments of Surrender

REVEALING THE MISSING PIECES

Charlene Bolden

Thank you for your Support!
Grace, peace, and God's
Richest blessings to
you!

Charlene Bolden

For information, contact:
moments4surrender@gmail.com

ISBN: 978-0692803899

TABLE OF CONTENTS

DEDICATION

My Heavenly Father, who has entrusted me with the privilege of sharing my story and undeniable passion for empowering women and young ladies globally. I surrender this book to effectively advance the Kingdom of God and His righteousness.

To every God-sent mentor and instructor in my life, you have invested, nurtured, and enlightened me with the Word of God and biblical based principles to help me walk into the fullness of what God has ordained for my life. Through you, I have learned the fundamental teachings that have sustained me and given me a reason to grow into the Christian woman I am today.

To all my friends and family who have supported, challenged, and offered encouragement. You have sown into my life the keys of surrender, humility, integrity, grace, and authenticity.

My church leaders, great instructors, and mentors have bestowed boundless wisdom and knowledge into my spirit, allowing me to navigate critical areas of my life effectively with a sense of diligence and humility. I carry an unfathomable feeling of appreciation and love for my many friends, and my church family for sustaining me on this path to womanhood. To each of them I express my sincerest gratitude and love.

PROLOGUE

Our lives are full of many seconds, minutes, hours, days, weeks and months that consist of moments that we remember. Spiritually, the moments that we have experienced, in relationship with God, help us to fully understand where we are now and where we are headed. Further, these moments condition us to think and absorb behaviors and mindsets. It's possible today to change the limiting beliefs and the dominating thoughts of your mind. Of all of the things I have lived through, the moments with God were so transforming that the manifestations, responses, encounters, and reactions allowed me to grasp a rich understanding of this concept. The moments of surrender that you have with the Holy Spirit will forever change the quality of the life you live. What I am about to share with you is not a system or formula, but a sure way to transform your entire destiny through wisdom, insight, information, and inspiration.

Every day that we wake up, we are all confronted with what is going on in our world. Every situation that we live through creates a reality of our world. If this reality is not aligned properly to God's will, then we ultimately undermine who we are. God always meets us where we are and knows where we are in our hearts and mind. Whether you are at the peak of success or experiencing hurt, betrayal, anger, frustration, abandonment, or family break-up. It is during those times that one must summon the inner strength and courage to press through the pain of it all and seek to embrace and fully release every area of your life to the Creator. This process of surrendering will not take place overnight but the process builds gradually and promotes appreciation, peace, happiness, love and contentment. When you respond to such truth, God radically transforms your life. In your transformation, you will find freedom and ease in the midst of both challenging and joyful experiences of life; moving from the paralysis of fear of the unknown and pretense of knowing to the giddying heights of having it all together. It's in those moments of surrender that you can fully experience the greatness that is birthed through your release!

As I began to write this book, I experienced great travail as the Holy Spirit began to "reveal and birth" these chapters. This book will breathe a message of unconditional surrender that is a work of the Holy Spirit. This spiritual journey has been difficult, sometimes painful and frustrating, and took years to work through. So read at your own pace, allow yourself to grasp every revelation regardless of how long it takes, and allow the Holy Spirit to work inside you. Let God move in His mysterious way to reconcile you with that place in your life where clarity and innocence is yours to behold. With the continuing presence of His spirit will come an understanding of the meaning of surrender to His will and the empowerment of humility. God's love is eternal and unconditional. For it to be manifested it demands trust, sacrifice, commitment and faith.

As you step into every moment of your surrender, embrace your truth; a moment that begins with a commitment to God first, giving everything over to Him without bounds. It is paramount to submit patiently to the Holy Spirit to fully understand each revelation of who He is and for the power of His work to come through the demonstration of his power in what He does. It is my prayer that what we do will perfectly reflect the truths that have been revealed to us at every stage of our lives through the moments that lead to our surrender.

Chapter One

EMBRACE YOUR VULNERABILITIES

But he who did not know and did things worthy of a beating shall be beaten with few [lashes]. For everyone to whom much is given, of him shall much be required; and of him to whom men entrust much, they will require and demand all the more. (Luke 12:48)

Are you the type of person who abhors wearing your emotions on your sleeve? Are you intent on maintaining an image of someone who "has it all together"? Or, have you cajoled everyone into not seeing the real you? On your journey towards surrender you must ask yourself, is there a longing for such deep connection with the Holy Spirit? How do you get in your own way? What do you want most out of life?

It all happened unexpectedly for me. I realized that God was birthing a message of "surrender" in me. Part of me wanted something more and deeper. It began as I started to examine areas of my spiritual development. The Holy Spirit began to deal heavily with me. I began to see that my passion was for the call that was on my life. I began to get paralyzed in fear and felt so heavy. God began showing me errors in my walk with Him. Things such as never wanting to be in the front, always devaluing my gifts, never sharing my testimony, and in some cases my unbelief. I had not fully surrendered my everything to him. I held back hurts, frustrations, and would ignore what God would speak to me. I battled being the first responder to His truths. In my mind, I wrestled with the emotions that come along with great responsibility and accountability. I knew deep down inside that it was going to be a journey that would cost me my entire life. I was in a spiritual battle within my heart and my mind. As I started to sit in silence, God began to reveal what was truly in my heart and mind. It was a lack of trust in His plan for my life. I had allowed the circumstances of my life to consume and weigh me down. God spoke to me, revealing that which I was seeking for in His presence and in my spirit, was closely connected to how much I released to Him. I had to give God everything—the good, the bad, and the indifferent.

As you embrace this concept of totally surrendering everything that you are and will be to the Father, it is imperative for you to recognize your most vulnerable areas. The moment of surrender is the point during which your vulnerabilities are revealed, exposed, and given to the Father. It requires a strong, courageous person to bare his or her true self. Before we deal with how you can move forward, it is important to identify the real issues. Think about where you get most discouraged. What gives you energy? What is holding you back? What are three changes right now that would move you closer to your desired life and spiritual connection with God?

Moments of surrender begin with transparency in attributing value to your relationship with God and the expectation of moving forward. The more you give to the Father, represents the higher value it is to your life. If your heart has been seeking for more, then get ready to move into another realm. If you are hungry for the manifestations of the Holy Spirit, then you must position yourself to give everything to Him. Often, the issues that leave you nurturing deep pain are the hardest to deal with; those that you just will not let go; those that center around what is spiritually lacking in your life. Beneath our smiles, we are often fighting an inner war which preempts the life of peace and healing that the Holy Spirit can bring.

Elevation to this level of peace and healing requires a conscious effort to forego thoughts and actions that promote feelings of anger, depression, unwillingness to forgive, as well as thoughts of suicide. The moment of surrender enhances the clarity of vision and conviction of the spirit necessary to look deeply and honestly into the underlying realities of one's life and psyche. This is not an easy task, but I can guarantee this will bring your greatest blessings, your most satisfying relationships, and will ultimately draw you towards a closer walk with God in a new direction.

Chapter Two

SURRENDERING - YOU CAN'T LOSE

Taking time to surrender your heart, mind and emotions in a safe place while spending quiet moments with God, gives you confidence to let go or relinquish whatever it is that is holding you back. These moments with God will allow you to see the things that are draining and distracting you from God's will for your life. These moments give God an opportunity to reveal His infinite wisdom that can eliminate these issues and bring back your focus. This paves the way for a level of intimacy with the Father that can sustain you. Allowing you to grasp hold of the level of insight that will lead towards the things of God. We must be willing to grow closer to God by surrendering every day.

Surrendering to the will of God allows you to show up in every moment of your life just as you truly are and allows the Spirit of God to mold and shape you into the person He has ordained you to become. He desires to show you results that flow from your authentic desires, strengths, and weaknesses and will then use these results to bring glory to His name and a spirit of change into your life. Surrendering all your vulnerabilities allows you to become present in every moment with God and opens you up to be honest with yourself creating room for growth and development.

Surrender is an act of the will, not of emotions. Emotions are continuously changing and unreliable in you. Your emotions invite interference and cause you to stand in your own way. However, surrender is a process that prepares the way for God to take full control of your life while giving you the confidence to walk into the power and freedom of the living God. This power gives you the strength and ability to recover and rise above any obstacles that are presented to you along the way.
He is calling us to rise again:

For a righteous man falls seven times, and rises again,
But the wicked stumble in time of disaster and collapse. (Proverbs 24:16)

Many of us have an idea of what we want to change about ourselves, but often we are overwhelmed by the steps necessary to affect such change. But now is NOT the time to be complacent, waiting for another opportunity to present itself to get it right, but rather a time to become proactive, to marshal the fortitude to combat despondency of spirit and weak-willed co-dependencies. I have come to the realization that God is calling for change on the inside. If you allow the Holy Spirit to deposit this revelation and understanding of surrender, God will bless you and strengthen you on your journey. Your heart and spirit will become newly transformed and you will never turn back. It is impossible to experience His grace, victory, and strength without first surrendering everything to God.

God declares, *I will give you a new heart and put a new spirit in you; I will remove from you your heart of stone and give you a heart of flesh. (Ezekiel 36:26)*

You will discover that having vacated this enervating place, you will be spiritually stronger for having gone through the experience. I assure you that when surrendering to the will of the Heavenly Father, you will thank Him for molding, guiding and positioning you to fulfill your destiny in life. The spirit of God will reach into the core of your being and facilitate your quest to walk in obedience to the calling on your life. Through His comfort and guidance, you will become refreshed. You will find that through Christ's ministry your past emotional wounds will be totally healed. There is nothing to lose when you submit to the will of God. Surrendering your imagined right of self-control in this way allows you to become free from burdensome attachments, personal insecurities, selfish detachments, and in some cases, free from a form of Godliness that denies the true power of God. Each moment of this surrender will bring you closer to the liberating love of Christ and remove the ugly distractions of negativity that preempt God's omnipotence as it relates to you.

When you feed into, and meditate on that which is 'wrong,' you will lose the time and ability to liberate your spiritual self as it was ordained. Liberty allows you invaluable 'thinking/working space' to realize and effectively take command of your 'flow' of gifts, callings, talents and purpose in life. NOW is the time to evict the detritus that precludes the will of God for your life from your heart, mind and body.

When you are consumed by the negative aspects of life that add pressure, remember that the enemy "*comes only to steal, kill and destroy.*" But Jesus came that you *"may have and enjoy life, and have it in abundance [to the full, till it overflows]."(John 10:10)*

It is important to never stop believing for the life and abundance that was promised to you. Continue to believe God to be a healer, a restorer and a sustainer. Always believe God to show you the paths of elevation to greater levels of insight, fresh perspectives, and His strength in your life. You must take back any ground that you have given the enemy and decide to believe God's word. **NOT THE ENEMY.** Worry and doubt tend to block us and while moving forward, we are hindered mightily without end. When we consciously ignore the power of positive thought, we do so to our own eternal peril. It is through the liberation found in God's plan for us that we will "eliminate the negative, accentuate the positive" and in the process, forget everything in between so that we may die to our flesh and depend solely on the Father's will for our lives.

The Holy Spirit enables us as we become open to this process. We begin adopting a renewed spirit regarding the acceptance of God in every moment of our lives. This girds you with strength and makes your way perfect granting you supernatural strength and abilities. Through your surrender and willingness to let go of negative feelings, perceptions, and thoughts concerning yourself, you can declare freedom from all influences, and repeating cycles passed down from one generation to another. You will be strong enough to resist every spirit that negatively affects your soul. You can release burdens, feelings of heaviness, oppression, and depression. God will begin to "*perfect those things concerning you.*" (*Ps.138:8*)

God declares in His word, *"Behold, I am making all things new." (Revelation 21:5)* This newness enables growth, promotes life-giving, indispensable energy that seeks out and extracts vile impurities from our spirits, adding a new approach to life and vanquishing the former spiritual conditions that confront us by day and haunt us by night. Suddenly, it is no longer in vogue to dwell on the things that are dead. If one decision to surrender everything has the power to release you, why are you not more liberated?

Your soul would become enlightened, fresh and new. The power of your decision has an ability to create an altar before God. This accelerates your process of releasing your life to the one with a greater plan and allows the condition of your heart to stay close to revival. Just as a house settles on its foundation, you may find little cracks and crevices that form because of the process. However, don't let the cracks discourage you in the process. The process excites the greater mindset to adopt a more efficient approach to the realm of greatness inside of you. The cracks stake claim to the character and beauty that are the milestones marking the process. Therefore, refrain from covering up or being ashamed of the cracks in your life! They represent the critical areas of growth. They reveal the wounds of honor that you bear, and witness to the accelerated moments of growth and unmitigated surrender of your will to the Creator.

A Creator who knows the foundation, the needs, and the desires that reside hidden in the recesses of your active imagination, understands all the attributes needed to transport the spirit to total truth and pristine righteousness. Be willing to go through the process. Sometimes, the most beneficial challenges carry the greatest risks, but as investors in the realm of the Spirit, you will need to take calculated risks. There is no failure in the plan of God as you have nothing to lose. See it as the greatest investment you will ever make. The most important thing to remember is that God's process will often humble us and direct our attention to Him. Surrendering to God says, *I trust my life in your hands. You God, ultimately know what is best for me.*

Surrendering allows you to partner with God's will for your life. It is akin to the tenets of marriage; as when a last name is taken, everything of the name-taker is bestowed upon the name-giver, and vice versa. Such is the way the domain of Christ will encapsulate your life. Everything that is His becomes YOURS. His desires, His heart, and His love. God wants us to be an equal partner to His will and His ways; not casually, but sincerely and completely. He wants a covenant relationship with you. He wants the Holy Spirit to mark you. He wants you to claim the full benefits of what He can offer you.

During this process, continue to seek the spiritual God; the everlasting God; the omnipotent God; a God revealed not through pomp and circumstance but in the glow of the humility emanating from your own soul and being in His presence.

Chapter Three

WHAT'S PULLING YOU AWAY?

He leads the humble in what is right, and the humble He teaches His way. All the paths of the Lord are mercy and steadfast love, even truth and faithfulness are they for those who keep His covenant and His testimonies. For your name's sake, O Lord, pardon my iniquity and my guilt, for [they are] great. Who is the man who reverently fears and worships the Lord? Him shall He teach in the way that he should choose. He himself shall dwell at ease, and his offspring shall inherit the land. The secret [of the sweet, satisfying companionship] of the Lord have they who fear (revere and worship) Him, and He will show them His covenant and reveal to them its [deep, inner] meaning. (Psalm 25:9-14)

Surrendering is a term that is widely used. However, very few have fully understood its ability to forever change lives. While we all need support, encouragement and accountability on this journey, our true success comes down to our time well spent in the presence of God and what we have released to Him. Rather than resent the lack of God's spiritual influence on our lives, we should cherish the opportunity to capitalize on whatever little of ourselves is ready to be in the presence of God.

Have you ever dreamed of what your life would be like if you were truly free from what you've been holding on to? Very often, simple thoughts, or certain situations that weigh on your heart will naturally force you to seek a place of freedom which is more conducive to spiritual change and receiving full benefit from the elusive words that plant spiritual understanding. This tugging and pulling is also God's way of making His presence evident, and His intention of empowering us with the strength and courage to deal with, and overcome our maladies, both physical and spiritual. The Holy Spirit will guide us to the place where we absolutely can surrender our total being to the will of the Father. At the point and place of 'ultimate' surrender, there is an absence of conscious force and a spirit of peace that accompanies the recognition of the opportunity to choose and serve Him. That sense of 'pulling and tugging' that seems to originate from 'a small, still voice,' now transforms itself into a deep-toned feeling of sensitivity to the Word (*truth)*, as the Spirit of God speaks to you, teaches you, and leads you.

Against this back drop of surrender and sensitivity, the negative forces, situations, and activities that once pulled you away from the truth and the will of God are now better visualized, in this pure light, as agents of mass spiritual destruction. Any subsequent attempt to tune out The Word of God becomes totally anathema to your new spiritual self. You will become exceedingly spiritually sure-footed as you walk with Him.

My former experience with tugging within me, and pulling on me often occurred during times when I allowed the entanglements of my past to verge and distract me from paying attention to the grace and purpose of God in my life. It was difficult for me to get to that next level of self-disclosure that facilitated the identification, enumeration and confrontation of past secret aspects of my existence that hindered me from truly and honestly acknowledging things that were distracting me. Many of the pleasures of the world; and of the flesh so distracted me that I did not know who I was!

Life in foster-care was one of the greatest experiences that led me to embrace this idea of surrender. I remember it so well because the experience became one of the most pivotal parts of my life, driving me for years to come; opening my eyes to the grace of God and increasing the capacity of my faith. It was one of those moments that seemed very difficult to digest. This moment blind-sided me, catching me off guard, and I began to feel uncomfortable with entering the foster care system and being taken away from my family. This experience was so traumatic and with every placement I could feel my face tensing up out of anger and frustration. Emotions that I never knew I had in me began to take over. I was trying to pick up the pieces of my life one piece at a time but somehow it became overwhelming. I was taken away from everything that I knew. Without any warning or time to prepare, I had to live with strangers, moving and packing frequently, and it was completely out of my hands. I was confronted with so many years of living as an outsider to those around. I was fearful of where I'd end up—what home and school would be next. This experienced gave me a tough outer shell to protect myself from more hurt and rejection. I understood that many did not quite understand the challenges of foster care. So many of my mentors would say this is going to get better and you will come out of this stronger than you've ever been.

As I went through the system, I lost my self-identity. I fought an ongoing battle to determine who I was. It was one of the most detrimental things a foster youth can face. With the experience of moving every holiday into a new home from the age of 13, I began to lose sense of who I was. I felt like I did not have a voice. The very life I dreamed of having fell apart. My experience of being separated from my siblings at one point caused me to feel unstable in my spirit and heart. These were my truths. As my world kept changing, I put a demand in my spirit that I would be all that I was ordained to be and would be free when it was my time.

Over the years I embarked on my life changing journey, and what a journey it was. It seemed that every time I'd start to build momentum, something else negative would occur. I went through a season of experiencing strongholds in relationships with others, while experiencing more and more hurt. I had a few moments during the process that made me want to quit altogether, but very few. I remember my twin sister offering words of encouragement during each of those moments. She would say, "Charla, God is going to change your life in His timing but you can't get bitter about this. You need to keep using your gifts. Don't let anyone move you out of that secret place with God."

I continued to be driven by seeking the face of God, hard work, and maintaining my integrity. During every moment as I continued to surrender to God's plan for me, I realized that on your journey you will see small victories and breakthroughs along the way that serve as reminders that God is with you. Never forget them because in His timing you will look up and your faith will be greater than you could imagine. You will be so strong and mature. This journey of surrender takes hard work and you will be so appreciative and humble when you finally get to where God ordained for you. You will know that it was the grace of God that gave you the courage to keep pressing. Remember, all of the work, all of the sacrifice, all of the setbacks will not matter when you cross over to the other side. I am so blessed beyond measure that throughout this season, God was nudging and challenging me. This revealed that there was a stretching that was occurring that strengthened my faith. The places of pain and brokenness in my life were a part of His plan. It set the tone for me to rely more and more on Him. I learned that my life in foster-care does not define me and that my soul can rest knowing that if I give control back to the one who created me, then I can be at peace with my situation. In those moments when you feel that the odds are stacked against you, or that you will collapse, the question that you should ask is "How will God get the glory?" This question forces you to search out the good in your situation.

I had finally reached a place where I needed to find a spiritual identity. It seemed that everything that had grown on me had become so much a part of me, that I didn't even realize it even existed. I carried the grief, pain and hurt of statements such as, "You will never be successful," or "You are bipolar and mentally unstable." Predictions that I would be another statistic of having an unwanted pregnancy or that I was "boy-crazy," remained with me. I remember being psychologically evaluated in one home where it was assumed that I was "developmentally delayed." The psychologist confirmed there wasn't anything mentally unstable after evaluating me and thought the foster parent had more of an issue. But despite all of what was said by those who had no real compassion for my situation, I began to pray. I began to rebuke the enemies' lies.

Those individuals were very selfish and had no inclination of what was going on in my head. I learned to seek God at an early age for super-natural faith. I was not concerned about looking to anyone to accomplish or give anything to me but looked to the one who created me. Growing up, so many people came up with excuses for not being in my life or sharing critical moments of my success with me. I felt ignored and unwanted and like an outsider to most around me. The wounds of rejection left me challenged spiritually. But, I found out through having supernatural faith that I would have to push past the barriers, and break every generational curse. I would be the voice to speak out. I would be the instrument of God's grace and love. I understood the struggle of moving into the unknown and entering a new level of thinking. At an early age, I began to believe God for vision, purpose and dreams. I began to believe God to push past the limits of my situation and embrace the true nature of who I was. I realized that God's anointing comes not always at times when situations were in my favor, but it was during those moments when I didn't expect greatness to be birthed, that it was in fact, birthed.

I felt rejected by my mother and abandoned by many others that I felt were supposed to be there for me. I carried the anger and resentment with me as I dealt with being split and shifted through the foster care system. The level of trust that had been broken in the mist of betrayal, hurt and disappointments became deadly markers that weighed me down. Any zeal for life slowly and inexorably dwindled away. The more I witnessed physical and sexual abuse in stifling and crowded living conditions, the more I was determined not to be another statistic. Someone who ended up pregnant, without any education, or a numbed human product of foster care. I felt as if the normality and innocence of my youth were stolen from me before I could fully understand them.

Despite the devastations, hurt, betrayal, and disappointments, I always maintained a passionate vision of hope for my future. I always believed in myself and my ability to succeed and improve. As a ward of foster care, I had to grow up quickly and as such, I didn't get to enjoy the experience of safety and security that was second nature to average youths of my age including holiday family dinners and a secure and loving environment. The absence of a permanent place to call home was a condition that broke me down in so many ways. Just transitioning through the many foster homes brought me in contact with unscrupulous individuals who only took me in for reasons of their own. This was utterly devastating in its feeling of hopeless abandonment. Nevertheless, the abandonment, rejections, disappointments, and abuse only steeled my resolve to better my condition and prepared me to become the strong woman that I am today.

All through my life in foster care, I was constantly placed with strangers. I had to adjust not only to different family situations, but to different locations, schools and new rules and regulations. Important decisions were made on my behalf by the courts, the social welfare agency and caretakers. For all intents and purposes, emotional and physical ties with my parents were non-existent. Undoubtedly this absence of basic parental emotional support, coupled with the stress and mental trauma inherent in foster care, denied me a stable environment. It was very difficult for me at this time not to be angry and I began to lash out. I learned the art of survival from placement after placement. I learned to be self-reliant and strong. In the process, I also learned to make an elixir of lemonade from the bitter lemons of life that were endlessly handed to me. At the age of 13, slowly and purposefully,

I began my search and ultimate surrender to God's teaching. Eventually, I discovered a stable source of love and spiritual support that allowed me to move beyond the challenges that dogged my life in foster care.

Living in a world of hurt from such an early age inevitably made me blame others. I fell into the trap of resigning others into prisons for the crimes they did not commit. I lived my daily life with my guard constantly up as a safeguard against anyone getting close enough to me to control me or hurt me. I was very angry; sometimes unreasonably so. At times, I would unleash that anger towards my aunt who made the 'good' calls concerning my family situation attempting to achieve an intervention to address the crushing lack of familial stability and trust which eventually strained the relationship with my siblings.

Somewhere along the way, it was revealed to me that the spirit of God wants to align His divine healing power with the secret cries of your heart. He wants to love you until you love yourself. He wants to heal you so that you will be able to see past all of the abandonments, addictions, lack of trust and excruciating spiritual hurt. The open wounds that you bear, and the embarrassments that attend you daily, will wash away and perish down the drain of His salvation.

I possessed a keen awareness of those who wore the symptoms of abuse, insecurity and vulnerability, as well as those who carried fear. I lacked regard for those who had walked away from my life. Those who had attacked me for reasons I was not even aware of. Those who had told me that I would never amount to anything and those who tried to play on my dreams and visions. In retrospect, through the divine presence of God, I see their worth in the grand scheme of my development. Subsequently, I have gained a greater appreciation for each of them.

My twin sister, who knows me better than anyone, could always tell something was wrong. She would say, "Charla, don't allow this to eat you up, and steal your joy. You are better than blessed."

Every time, I would look at her with my eyes glossy, trying to hold back the tears in my anger and simply say, "I won't stop believing for my change."

During one of those moments, I experienced conflicting emotions warring within me. I was both extremely happy for where I was, yet extremely disappointed about how my life was playing out. But something was different while I was in this moment. I felt that little voice inside of my spirit telling me, "You can get through this. "Your dreams can be your reality, and nothing is impossible."

I can't explain what happened, but I felt in my spirit that God was giving me power and strength to think bigger, embrace the idea of possibility, and accept with His permission, that my situation was for His glory. At this moment, I couldn't even wait to spend time with God, in hopes that I would hear more of what

He had to say to my heart. No longer do I sit and think *there is something wrong with me*, or that *I am incapable of finding my own voice because of previous life-altering circumstances*. Now I am comforted in knowing that I am the apple of God's eye, and that beyond my layers of brokenness, I have an indomitable will that had been dormant but is now fully awake.

A person who has experienced the negative aspects of life that carry varying degrees of hurt, may be unaware of the attendant blessings that escape those who are fortunate enough to be shielded from such trials and tribulations. The greatest blessing is the testimony of God's glory that will always be with you. Others will see in your spirit, the majestic power of His presence. The presence of the hand of God that now lifts you. The sovereignty of God able to help you survive against the odds and comfort you in the eye of the storm.

If you set your heart aright and stretch out your hands to [God], If you put sin out of your hand and far away from you and let not evil dwell in your tents; Then can you lift up your face to Him without stain [of sin, and unashamed]; yes, you shall be steadfast and secure; you shall not fear. For you shall forget your misery; you shall remember it as waters that pass away. And [your] life shall be clearer than the noonday and rise above it; though there be darkness, it shall be as the morning. And you shall be secure and feel confident because there is hope; yes, you shall search about you, and you shall take your rest in safety. You shall lie down, and none shall make you afraid; yes, many shall sue for your favor. (Job 11:13-19)

It is important that you acknowledge within yourself that despite the negative, difficult and painful things of your past, that past does not carry the power to dictate your destiny or determine your relationship to God. This passage of scripture promises that at the moment of surrendering our hearts to the Father, the moment you stop doing the things that separate you from the Father, will be the moment you lift up your face and will stand firm, without fear. Fear is a distraction that is used to prevent you from movement. Fear causes you to miss the mark in terms of opportunities because it hems you up. It distorts your sense of value and purpose and entangles you, limiting your ability to attain the success that is available to you. Figuratively, the advantage of dealing with fear is that it cleans out your spiritual closet in the recesses of your heart, spirit, body, and soul which may remain stagnant. Fear clutters your spirit from accessing the realm of greatness that belongs to the Father.

Think about what's in your closet. What frustrations and nuances, and areas of defeat are hanging in the back of your closet? What causes the clutter and undermines your success, energy or productivity?

As you think about that for a moment, think about what things you can surrender. Let go of things that have cluttered your life in your immediate environment. Are these things slowing you down?

What I have learned throughout my journey is that this clutter causes you to become highly inefficient and dysfunctional. In some instances, it may even cause you to self-destruct, become toxic and kill your destiny. Clutter causes you to lose energy in the present because you are now focused on the distraction instead of the purpose. In this season, it's my prayer that you take time to clean out your spiritual and personal closets. That you rid yourself of the old mindset, and ways of doing things that prevent you from performing intentionally with greater focus, power, and wisdom. Isn't this what God would want anyway?

As you embrace that process, God will give you strength to look forward to better times. He will bless you with healing and change your perspective about your circumstances. The past will be as "*as waters that pass away.*" When God is moving you to experience this realm of surrender, often there is something that He begins to birth in you. With this movement in the spiritual realm, the enemy will do whatever he can to distract, discourage, defeat and defuse you to take your mind from the plan of God. The enemy is intentional and crafty in making you think that the damage will always remain or that you will be forever stuck with the memory of it. Satan attacks whatever dreams, hopes and plans we desire in hopes that we will dwell in anguish, bitterness, depression and distress beyond what we feel we can bear. The truth is, you cannot move forward if you're always looking back at your past! Now is the time to be transparent with God in all honesty. Invite Him into the crevices of your heart. So, what are you holding on to? What is God asking you to let go of?

KNOW THE FOLLOWING:

1. **THE DECISION TO SURRENDER WILL TEND TO BE THE MOST DIFFICULT AT FIRST.**

If you are going to fully commit your life, you cannot allow yourself to focus on all that will be required as you let go. Don't allow this journey to intimidate you. You have more in you than you could ever imagine. Everything that you release is attached your victory. Don't back up from this process because of fear. Remember that the places you fear the most are the places, when fully surrendered, will bring you the greatest victory.

2. **JUST BECAUSE IT DOESN'T LOOK THE WAY YOU WANT IT TO DOESN'T MEAN IT'S NOT GOD'S PLAN FOR YOUR LIFE.**

Even in the mist of difficult times in our lives, our process at times will leave us broken, wounded, and deceived to think that we will never be able to recover. You slowly lose your zeal and fire for God. You begin to slowly but surely shrink back to your old way of doing things and coping. You step out of the place of strength and spiritual protection. Eventually, you stop believing and become cold hearted for fear of experiencing the same pain.

Yet, you must remember to keep moving forward, keep believing and hoping. You may feel like you've run out of strength and the will to trust again or dream again, but when you surrender all of this, you have a place of victory in Christ. You must be able to challenge with faith and trust in God the things that are trying to shut you down and discourage you. Even when situations make you think that your dreams have died or when you have lost hope, God can revive you, strengthen you, and use you. There is purpose in your pain. Nothing will ever go wasted. The greater the pain, the more it is an indication of a sensitive area that God wants you to fully release to Him. Once released, He can allow His healing and transformation to begin. After that process, you may have some scars but you've been healed and released. God's plan for your life is effective and will prosper and equip you.

2 Chronicles 7:14-16 declares:

"*If My people, who are called by My name, shall humble themselves, pray, seek, crave, and require of necessity My face and turn from their wicked ways, then will I hear from heaven, forgive their sin, and heal their land. Now My eyes will be open and My ears attentive to prayer offered in this place. For I have chosen and sanctified (set apart for holy use) this house, that My Name may be here forever, and My eyes and My heart will be here perpetually.*"

3. **WHEN YOU HEAR THAT STILL SMALL VOICE…ARISE.**

Take a moment to reflect on the many thoughts and ideas that cross your mind. Have you acted on them? What is getting in between you and your desired outcome? I realize that the time is NOW to act on what you have in you. Don't let it be just another an idea for someone else. The thing that often prevents us from experiencing the power of God in those areas is the time that you allow to pass before you move forward and release. You must be willing to diligently obey the voice of the Lord your God.

4. **DECIDE TO COMMIT YOUR LIFE TO GOD.**

I've learned to accept the will of God and I constantly say, "Lord, have your way with my life." Continue to "*Commit your way to the Lord [roll and repose each care of your load on Him]; trust (lean on, rely on, and be confident) also in Him and He will bring it to pass.*" *(Psalm 37:5)* When you do, everything that you put your hands to do will be established and will succeed. *(Prov.16:3)* Choose to believe in the One greater who will prove to be stronger in every circumstance that you see or situation that you face. C*ontinually "refute arguments and theories and reasonings and every proud and lofty thing that sets itself up against the [true] knowledge of God;" and "lead every thought* *and purpose away captive into the obedience of Christ."* (2 Cor. 10:5) The bible declares "*Do not fret or have any anxiety about anything, but in every circumstance and in everything, by prayer and petition, with thanksgiving, continue to make your wants known to God. And God's peace [shall be yours]*. We are encouraged to think on positive things, "*whatever is true, whatever is worthy of reverence and is honorable and seemly, whatever is just, whatever is pure, whatever is lovely and lovable, whatever is kind and winsome and gracious, if there is any virtue and excellence, if there is anything worthy of praise, think on and weigh and take account of these things [fix your minds on them]*. (Phil. 4:6-9) On your journey, rely solely on God. Every time I've trusted God, God never failed me. Surrender says, "*despite all of my options, I chose you and I am willing not to go after anything in my own strength*."

5. FINALLY, GOD IS A STRATEGIST WITH A PLAN AND PURPOSE FOR YOUR LIFE.

Nothing happens by accident. God allows your moments of surrender to challenge you because of the mark of distinction that he wants to give you. He wants to give you easy access to His tools to help you with every situation. God's strategy is always to get the glory. He sets you apart for His strategy to move you further and to perfect you. There is great power, anointing and authority that comes when you align with His will. Your surrender brings you closer to the doors He is about to open, the connections you are about to make, and the healing that you desire in your life. Don't go another day questioning your life any further. God's got you.

1 Corinthians 2:9 declares: *"as the Scripture says, What eye has not seen and ear has not heard and has not entered into the heart of man, [all that] God has prepared (made and keeps ready) for those who love Him who hold Him in affectionate reverence, promptly obeying Him and gratefully recognizing the benefits He has bestowed."*

It is through your transparency that much of your moments of surrender will be communicated and accepted in the presence of God. It is time for you to allow God to carry you further. Surrendering allows you to reach deep down inside yourself to access the new level, possibility and solutions the spirit of God has for you. Whether your heart has been broken because of shattered relationships, broken promises, or the painful memories of being taken advantage of; whether you have experienced sickness or whatever the case may be, now is not the time to give up!

Maybe you are still living in your past. Perhaps, dealing with loneliness or a deep desire to fit in somewhere. No matter the circumstance, God has your back and will give you the power to overcome your worst day. The Holy Spirit has an uncanny way of focusing your attention, changing the way you feel about a situation or person, and prompting you to make the choice every day to let go and move forward. You will begin to take actions not previously considered because they were blocked from your awareness. Whether you were sexually violated, or otherwise abused by someone you trusted. Whether you were treated as if you never existed or told that you were the black sheep of the family. For those whose dreams were crushed before they were even conceived; for those who tried to over compensate for the lost that was felt; for those who tried so hard to forget the words that hurt the most, now is the time to know a life of being free. It's now time for you to step over the barriers that have tried to block you and to rise above your past! If you think you must stand in prayer lines to get it, read books on it, or listen to speeches on it, you are sadly mistaken. The core of your being will expose the deepest truth that giving in to the Holy Spirit will break down anything that negatively affects you. You were created with everything that you need to break this cycle. You no longer must continually waste time and energy in unproductive relationships, or take on destructive behaviors to hide behind the pain, or condemn yourself for the times that you have been deceived.

Sometimes we are rocked so hard by life's circumstances that the very preciousness of life can neither be felt nor expressed. In extreme cases, we become numb. Over time, it becomes evident that mature spiritual growth is a process. It is a process that is wholly positive which facilitates profound personal growth and brings into sharp focus our vision of God as The Almighty.

The question becomes this. What happens in the absence of the saving grace of mature spiritual growth during the times when things are rough and rocky? My experience has taught me that you force yourself to give credence to the contorted belief that if you somehow endure long enough without complaint, there will be some sort of victory on the other side. Back then, when I thought about the place where I should be in life, or where I would end up, I became intimidated by my thoughts and grew frustrated. I had no desire to contemplate how changed my life would be if I submitted to the ordained purpose for my life. But in time, I learned to let go of that wounded spirit. I chose spirituality and God's word to eradicate the scars that seared so deeply into my being and I just trusted the reality of the one true living God.

The reality is this: that everything that you've suffered, endured, and every moment that you felt emptiness, or inadequacy, is the perfect opportunity to embrace the truth in ways that can turn things around. Now is the time to admit that you can't make it in this world without the manifest power of God. You were created for a special purpose.

In my case, the spiritual truth was what mattered and what I desperately held on to. During the most negative conditions, regardless of how I felt, or how hopeless it seemed, the only thing that mattered was the truth. My truth was that I was determined to be victorious. Though I felt lost to the point where the daunting task before me seemed impossible to overcome, I would never give up. Ultimately, I was forced to take a deeper look within to prepare and position myself to search for, and extract, the very best of myself that I could find.

Growing up I was exposed to struggle and abuse. You might say I was almost broken at an early age. These exposures made me feel like an abject failure, a failure without hope of ever living any of the dreams that were placed in my heart and mind. I vividly remember feeling that my life was being snatched away by the comments that people would make to, and about me. Looking back, these comments viciously attacked any ordained purpose in my life. I felt lost. Not surprisingly, I strayed from the path that was set before me. In actuality, my personality was utterly compartmentalized into a mystery of who I was, a personality that was an enigma because the components of my true identity were lost. Although I was that girl who appeared to have it all together, there were wounds that struggled to heal. The effort to suppress anger, hurt and abandonment led me to seething bitterness; a form of bitterness that was eroding and destroying the vision of the unique person I was determined to become. It was increasingly difficult to ascribe the line between living and existing. It was increasingly difficult to fill the voids of life and to lessen its blows. But it was in the pain from these storms that I found the strength needed to embrace the purest truth. Truth brings to the surface the spectra of the bad habits and self-destructive behaviors that are the narcotics which numb the cruel pains of life, and fill its void's silent emptiness.

I endeavored to forge a relationship with God nourished with a strong sense of peace, wisdom and strength. God spoke to me one time and I never thirsted again. I recall this as if it occurred yesterday. I stood face to face with my pain. I got on my knees one night in my shower and as the water began to flow all over me, I prayed fervently. I prayed for an encounter, an epiphany that would forever change my heart. I prayed for a circumcision of my heart, that the things that were pulling me away from the path set before me would be dissolved. I was determined that I would not get up until the spirit of God showed up right where I left all of my tears and all of my pain. I was intentional. As I prayed, I began to experience the presence of God. I began to get revelation concerning my situation from the Holy Spirit. God gave me a refreshing solution for every problem that I faced. As I sat there for hours, I experienced the power of release. I knew that somewhere I had gotten it wrong, that I could not control what happened to me, and that it was not my fault. I began to understand that now I'd have to allow the Holy Spirit to take over my inner woman. As I continued to sit, tears flowing, I don't know what I said in that prayer that caused the spirit of God to show up, but I remember saying, "God, I surrender all of me to you. You can have my heart, life, and my will. I can't do anything in this place. I can't trust anyone with my heart. I can't trust anyone, but God, I decide today to trust You."

I declared that day in the shower, that I would walk in supernatural faith. As I declared this, my spirit immediately felt lighter. I felt so much peace come over my body. I began to feel so warm on the inside, like that of a fire that had welled up in me. I felt on fire. I felt joyful. I felt victorious. I felt courageous and daring. It was one moment in my life that even shocked my twin sister. She says to me all of the time, "It was scary and transformative and I knew that you would never be the same." She knew that it was God's spirit at work within me.

What I want to share is that after you have taken a deeper look within; and after you have sought out the root cause of that which has left you so wounded, you will realize that the strength of God's word will help to overcome spiritual obstacles and heal life's maladies.

During periods of hurt or emptiness, it is natural to search for things to fill those areas but somehow I managed instead to search feverishly for God's presence and Spirit. Understand, there is an important subtle difference between searching for His presence and seeking His presence. One may search and never find, but to seek presupposes an attitude of submission and supplication which are elements more conducive to finding.

In addition, searching feverishly and not finding in a timely manner fosters frustration, distraction and temptation. Any one of which can subvert to best intentions and redirect them to the highs of unsavory, destructive behaviors and addictions. As you probably have seen in those suffering with an addiction, more and more of the drug is consumed to get higher and higher. However, God or the Spirit or salvation is never contemplated or sought. Unfortunately, addictive drugs only address symptoms and mask root causes. In this regard, drinking alcohol, popping pills, smoking and using illegal drugs may seem attractive and even fashionable, but you can't drown or drink your sorrows away. After the erotic high of every hard drug binge, there comes the crash; sickness; the emptiness of the morning after; and the harsh reality of a creeping, unrelenting doom. It's easy to blow past the ugly danger of physical dependency and think, "Hey, why not use again?" The addiction becomes the spirit that entices the belief that this is the way to escape from all present problems. When you find yourself at life's moment of truth, do you retreat and become isolated and negative? Or do you seek God to teach you what He wants you to learn in the midst of your situations? I promise you if you seek Him, He will speak to you on how to respond.

Early on I faced so much disappointment and depression that I fell into a critical state. I began to see things through the eyes of one abused. What seemed normal for some was morbidly strange to me. I was unable to appreciate those who were brought into my life to enhance my virtues and strengthen my weakness. It seemed so alien to what I had become accustomed to, that it felt like an attack upon my intellect.

Growing up, it was difficult to envision myself as a leader, even as I overcame early adversity. I was quite concerned about what was going on in my life and overlooked the possibility that God could have use for me. But in my desire and thirst for knowledge, I realized how God will use mysterious ways to reach us and nurture us. My truth was that God may not always want to utilize our most positive and formidable selves, but wants to engage us in some task where His wisdom, strength and power can be manifested to their utmost so as to bring light and healing to weak areas, the very areas about which we are most humiliated and ashamed to expose. God always wants us to project towards the future and our destiny. Often, knowledge and experience alone are not enough. We must be willing and open to receive the spiritual truths in our own hearts. It all started with my original mindset. I had to ask God to heal my mind to understand that although the pieces of my life were broken at that moment in time, I had to trust God's judgment for calling me out of my circumstances and adding foster-care to my life as a destiny-defining step.

Chapter Four

MOTIVES OF THE HEART!

"The plans of the mind and orderly thinking belong to man, but from the Lord comes the [wise] answer of the tongue. All the ways of a man are pure in his own eyes, but the Lord weighs the spirits (the thoughts and intents of the heart). Roll your works upon the Lord [commit and trust them wholly to Him; He will cause your thoughts to become agreeable to His will, and] so shall your plans be established and succeed." (Proverbs 16:1-3)

Did you know that God can see the deep and hidden areas in your life that are closed off from those that are around you? He can see the inner thoughts, secret cries and desires that no one knows are deeply hidden in your heart and mind. We at times can experience lapses in judgment or indulge in things that are outside the will of God and yet have a heart that wants to pursue righteousness. There were times in my heart and mind, where I wanted to live up to the challenge of maintaining a heart before God and I wanted God to show me why I would respond or react the way that I did.

You have to understand that the more you are accountable and in tune with that place inside you where your mind is constantly weighing various options, examining your ways before Him goes deeper than just your behavior. The spirit of God will reveal to you why you do what you do. This examination process uncovers the dark areas of the heart and will bring to the surface the insecurities, vulnerabilities, issues and motives of your heart.

Jeremiah 17:9 -10 declares*: "The heart is deceitful above all things, and it is exceedingly perverse and corrupt and severely, mortally sick! Who can know it [perceive, understand, be acquainted with his own heart and mind]? I the Lord search the mind, I try the heart, even to give to every man according to his ways, according to the fruit of his doings."*

I am sure that at some point you have met someone who has fallen into depression, or who has become bitter by reason of inflicted wounds. Each of us has issues that need to be addressed urgently. These are the types of issues that create vital blockages in key areas of our energy centers that are supposed to feed the spiritual heart. Such blockages subvert the flow of true peace of mind or contentment. Only a determined, self-motivated person can carry on despite overwhelming, stifling hardship and trauma. Nowadays, it almost appears normal for a person to be confronted with having to deal with unresolved spiritual and mental problems that keep their hearts heavy and their dispositions fragile. These events can crush any enthusiasm for life and trap a psyche into an endless cycle of depression.

Undoubtedly a person may change how they appear on the outside and 'get over' their world as it exists; but on the inside, if the motives of the heart are suspect, anger, bitterness, un-forgiveness, or resentment, a false sense of happiness will reign supreme. This will set up a dichotomy of pressurized possibilities; to forgive or to release, to use or abuse, to dream or to overcome. Motives are the underlying primal intentions of the heart. By motives, one may feed off certain spirits that promote acting in or out of character.

For example, I was once engaged in a situation that required working with a team of individuals on a project. Instinctively, I became aware of a feeling of uneasiness that emanated from my spirit during a first round of conversations about the project. It became evident later that my uneasiness was triggered by jealousy on the part of the other participants threatened by my willingness and enthusiasm to engage positively to achieve success. I could see clearly the real intentions behind the spirit through which the individuals were operating. They purposely would not help me because they felt I would surpass them. He will allow the foibles in others to be exposed and made known in subtle ways to those whose hearts He has cleansed and now inhabits.

If one's motives are pure, they will move to a place of truth. Motives will determine if one is nakedly materialistic; if one is entangled in the roots of bitterness, lacks empathy and appreciation for others, or is indulging in a continual cycle of chasing after things which are outside of God's will and domain. There is no doubt about the powerful effect of motives. Beyond their intention and capability of producing evil desires, is their utter genius at obfuscating which motives to embrace, to dwell on, and which ones to resist. As the purer motives are embraced with our heart and mind, the more negative and ungodly motives will be jettisoned. Those motives that are buried beyond the depth of secrecy are especially dangerous; even if their bent may be considered positive. That veil of secrecy can negatively influence the perception of others. Unfortunately, this is one of the elemental aspects of a personality that friend and foe alike will use to disgrace and to humiliate.

Right now it's time to dig up the things that hold you captive to mediocrity, procrastination or dead weight. The unwillingness to confess and go further breeds denial. You can't come to the light and not expect your darkness within to be exposed. God will invade your heart with a power and light that will project in stark contrast against the content of your character. Any experience with adulterous affairs, false pretenses, bad credit, overspending and issues related to pregnancy, molestation, rape, and abuse will flow like a turbulent river emptying itself in a mighty ocean. The motives of your heart will expose every spirit and correct what has become a terrible situation. Examining yourself to unlock some things supernaturally will give you a peace that you never experienced before. God desires to infiltrate your lives with His pure intentions and motives. When you have been a victim, you see the world through the eyes of a victim. The biggest trick the enemy uses is to get you wrapped up in the victim mentality. The motives of your heart can cause you to live successfully or foolishly. There are motives that perpetuate problems that can only take you but so far. Releasing your heart from the negative motives will allow you to embrace the truth in a way that can help you get down to the root of things that disrupt your life.

Chapter Five

GROWING PAINS PRODUCE GREATNESS!

For You, Lord, will bless the [uncompromisingly] righteous [him who is upright and in right standing with You]; as with a shield You will surround him with goodwill (pleasure and favor). (Psalm 5:12)

Now is not a time to give up! It's a time to seek the power and voice of God. I experienced an incredible encounter with the Holy Spirit that showed me a glimpse of what life in freedom would be for me. It was difficult for me to accept how greatness could be part of my destiny. I had allowed the growing pains of my past to hinder me from grasping the riches in glory, tender mercies and immeasurable favor that God had given me. I found that I was coming to a place where I had to conquer the demonic forces that were trying to pull me into dark places to incapacitate me and to silence the voice within. I had to announce my awareness to the plan God had for me. I refused to deny what rightfully belonged to me!

There were jaw clenching moments where I was left shaking my head after accruing countless issues within my relationships and friendships with others. Many times, I look back on my previous relationships and thank God for stepping in at the right time. His divine intervention ceased all distractive, disturbing, and destructive actions that controlled my thoughts, inspiration, revelation, insight, wisdom, knowledge, and understanding.

There were a couple relationships and friendships that I thought would last. Instead the relationship ended. Those that walked out of my life left me with a void that warranted closure for figuring out why it didn't work out and letting it go. For me, I was acquainted with the feeling of abandonment by my mother. So when others in my life walked out for reasons of their own selfishness, I had to depend on the assurance I had in Christ. As difficult as it is to deal with the same people who hurt you and act as if what they did was right, I had to develop an understanding of God's purpose for my life and gain perspective on why things turned out the way it did.

Many of us lack the robust understanding of God's divine intervention and how it can bring us in to His will. We see ourselves exempt from suffering and struggle, but when it occurs, we fail to see it for our own benefit. I had to mature in the word, to understand that the spiritual aspects of my journey were allowed by God to preserve and protect me. The understanding that God gave me was that I had to learn to see how God's hand was on my life, and to know that God's presence was there during all my circumstances. His presence helped me trust in Him more and to never to put my trust in man completely.

Often when we lose someone important, we tend to want to isolate our true feelings of abandonment and anger that invade our thoughts and emotions. We even walk around as if the loss did not even affect us. I often saw how God would send angels into my life at every transition. When people were making their exit, and would not look back, God always had someone prepared and entrusted with a miracle, or He used someone to bring words of encouragement and in many cases, closure and an understanding of why the situation at the time ended that way.

My life in foster care consisted of moving into different homes and being exposed to a lot. In my own life, I can honestly say that out of the deepest pain and disappointment has come the strongest conviction of the presence of God and the love of God. God's presence was real and at work even in the most discouraging times. I have learned that I can own this truth.

Through the Holy Spirit who lives inside of you, God is present and real. The hurt and pain at times can be difficult to bear but I have learned to appreciate the things that could have happened but did not. I developed a dependence on God for patience in the times when my back was against the wall. There were moments when I experienced many relationships on the rocks that were unhealthy and were a hindrance. I remember the Holy Spirit giving me a strong inner peace and a prompt reminder to rest with dependence on the guidance of the Lord. The power of Christ at work in my life, allowed me to identify and overcome any and every plan established for my demise.

People look at me today and mistake my confidence for arrogance. But throughout all my circumstances, I have been able to maintain a stable confidence in our faithful God and Father that He will meet my every need and turn what was meant for my bad, meant to bring depression and anger or any adversity my way, around for my good. In times, when I experienced sexual violations, a breach of trust, betrayal, times of deep distress, or a broken heart, I could rest knowing that God would reverse the effect of any stigmas and behaviors that came about as a result that I let go of. He would not allow me to go through anything he did not think I could handle.

He will move you continually to the place of divine closure, to understand the solutions available to you. You can trust the hand of God at work in your life. There were times when I would put myself in situations that I could not see were not a part of my destiny. God's grace and mercy followed me in those areas. Because of my desire to live according to the will of God, He would divinely intervene and cause those things to fall apart. He would never let anything happen and if I was on the verge of falling into something, there was always a change of plans. While others would have taken this situation as something negative, I was grateful and relieved. God loves us so much that He will work in the details of your life. It was through these times that I learned to adjust and become flexible. I learned to embrace the truth that everything will not always follow a schedule, or be planned, or flow or make sense to us because of the leading of the spirit. God will use the smallest things to get our attention because He loves us just that much!

As I caught on to the vision for my life and realized that where God was taking me was going to be great, I still had some unresolved issues I had refused to deal with. I did not want to understand the valleys I had to go through, the mountains I had to climb, nor the tears and pain I had to push through. But it was in these moments that I learned the power to surrender my entire will to the Father. It was in those times that the conditions of my heart were tested. My heart was so heavy and fragile that to spiritually be who I am, I had to decide to let go of everything that was holding me back. I had to understand that the valley experiences, were not because God didn't love me, or that I was the problem, but they were for me to see that in my weakest moments, surrendering to the will of God won me my greatest victories. I learned that in my weaknesses, God could truly perfect me, nurture me, and expand me in ways I never thought were possible. During the valley experiences or the moments of deep depression, my inner woman was being skillfully and strategically molded into the earthen vessel I am today. God had to use this experience to create in me a clean heart and renew a right spirit in me. I learned in these moments that God's sovereignty was necessary for me to grow. Whatever is stopping you must go!

Chapter Six

RESPOND WITH POWERFUL COUNTER REACTIONS

Therefore also now, says the Lord, turn and keep on coming to Me with all your heart, with fasting, with weeping, and with mourning [until every hindrance is removed and the broken fellowship is restored]. Rend your hearts and not your garments and return to the Lord, your God, for He is gracious and merciful, slow to anger, and abounding in loving-kindness; and He revokes His sentence of evil [when His conditions are met. (Joel 2:12-13)

As you are obedient to the first step, He will guide you. You have to make a conscious effort to move forward in your life at all times. When I went through all that I went through, I felt obligated to help those who didn't have the strength to move forward in life. I was surrounded by people who started to deplete me and become hindrances to me as I navigated the places He had for me. I learned that everyone around you is not always prepared for your destiny. I came out of dysfunction and mess. There was always confusion and drama surrounding me to the point to where there were life draining spirits attempting to follow, conceal, and warp me. I was exposed to those who had a hidden agenda.

In my moments of surrender, I learned that everyone with you is not always for you. It is now important that as you embrace the truth, know there are things in your life that seek to destroy you, hindering you from going into the place God ordained for you. You have to watch things that were never intended to follow you. There are habits, destructive language, attitudes, behavioral tendencies and wrong mentalities that slowly but surely will pull you down. There is always negativity that is born in the face of possibility. The spirit of the Lord wants to deal with every obstruction, hindrance, and disturbance until you let go of them. The circumstances in life are to build you up and bring you closer to things that God wants to show you. Often, when we are moving out of familiarity, we are uncomfortable. We begin to doubt. This is the time for faith to kick in.

"But our way is not that of those who draw back to eternal misery (perdition) and are utterly destroyed, but we are of those who believe [who cleave to and trust in and rely on God through Jesus Christ, the Messiah] and by faith preserve the soul.." (Hebrews 10:39)

Some things cannot be seen until they are released. This release will result in a severance of the spirit operating the persons or things with whom you have been connected. When He gives you revelation, it is to lift you up, leading you to peace and prosperity.

"Then shall your light break forth like the morning, and your healing (your restoration and the power of a new life) shall spring forth speedily; your righteousness (your rightness, your justice, and your right relationship with God) shall go before you [conducting you to peace and prosperity], and the glory of the Lord shall be your rear guard." (Isaiah 58:8)

God wants you to possess the fundamental truth of separation from every hindrance. If God is implementing a separation, a truth often will follow because He knows your future and walks with you into it. You can look forward and anticipate a spirit of change that will remove anything that is toxic and hindering you from getting to the place you desire.

Job 22:28 declares: *"You shall also decide and decree a thing, and it shall be established for you; and the light [of God's favor] shall shine upon your ways."*

As you prosper more and more each day, you will be strategically positioning yourself to obtain new hope, new life, new beginnings, and in faith, travel the journey God has for you toward joy as you learn and grow. You will be graced and poised in strength to make the most of every moment in your life.

Chapter Seven

SEVER TIES WITH THE OLD, UNHEALTHY HABITS, AND MINDSETS!

And set your minds and keep them set on what is above (the higher things), not on the things that are on the earth. (Colossians 3:2)

Our life fully surrendered to God includes everything from our mind, body and soul. This means that those things that once controlled us, or those things we were addicted to, must be surrendered. All those things which are sinful in nature, we become slaves to and eventually soul-tied to. They become a part of us and are usually very difficult to change without living intentionally to change them. The more we attempt to change them, the more they will try to remain.

There are 4 key steps to breaking the old mindsets and unhealthy habits:

1. Acknowledge

The first step with changing anything during the process of surrendering is acknowledging that there is something preventing you from being physically, mentally, and spiritually free. There is a problem that needs to be dealt with. I encourage you to make a list of the destructive things that you would like to change. Even in relationships, ask the Lord to show you who you need to let go of, or what issues you are holding on to, or reveal some of your personal pains that create the problems you have in the first place.

2. Swallow Your Pride: Confess and Repent

Staying in a state of repentance allows us to honestly acknowledge areas of weakness or the need for improvement. This will enable us to see the things that truly cause our downfall or allow us to fall short in the presence of God. This part of the process begins first in the presence of God.

> *But without faith it is impossible to please and be satisfactory to Him. For whoever would come near to God must [necessarily] believe that God exists and that He is the rewarder of those who earnestly and diligently seek Him [out].* (Hebrews 11:6)

When you go to Him, you invite His spirit and presence into this area to expose anything that is contrary to His will. Once you've done that, confess to God first, yourself second, and then any parties involved. For example, if you are dealing with issues in your relationship, you would first start with God and allow Him to reveal his instructions for correcting the situation. Then, you go to the individual(s) involved, apologize and remain accountable for your actions. Many individuals miss the opportunity to correct the situations in this part of the process because it does not feel good. The things that we are most ashamed of, or have made a mess of, are humiliating, embarrassing and in some cases shameful. We tend to shy away from these things but this is the key to the surrendering process. It's not about looking good, or even being right. It's about honestly acknowledging and taking responsibility for your part in the matter. When you fully relinquish your will to the Father, you will begin to see His spirit humble you and intervene. When we are in this state, we are humbler and God, in the end, can truly show up. But if we continually want to give the person a piece of what we are thinking, and allow our pride to step in, we will make the situation worse. Key criteria: there should be peace at this state. If it's anything else, then start back at Step 1.

3. Forgive

First accept God's forgiveness, then forgive yourself, and then anyone else involved. Not being able to forgive someone still means that you want to own the right to be upset, angry, and avoid the correction that forgiveness can bring. Un-forgiveness is so toxic to your mindset and patterns of behavior that it can prevent you from living your life freely. This part of the process helps you to see the other person as God sees them and not as you want to see them.

4. Develop a strong Prayer life

Prayer is one of the most powerful things you can do to ensure you are fully living a surrendered life. When you pray you are declaring, with your mouth, the power of Christ exposing any undermining efforts or initiatives against your life. This places emphasis on areas for which you desire His help. A prayer life is the channel through which God can speak to you, providing wisdom and making room for you to reflect on your actions. This keeps you in tune with the correct frequency of the Spirit.

Chapter Eight

EXPOSE THE FILTERS, FILLERS, AND VOIDS!

"If you set your heart aright and stretch out your hands to [God], If you put sin out of your hand and far away from you and let not evil dwell in your tents; Then can you lift up your face to Him without stain [of sin, and unashamed]; yes, you shall be steadfast and secure; you shall not fear." (Job 11:13-15)

Many of us have a void in life that we attempt to fill with either positive or negative people or activities. In my experience, on the outside these individuals appear to be have it all together, a fancy car, name brand clothes, or even a good job, but on the inside, is a gaping hole that they are attempting to fill. Whether you grew up in a home where love was conditional based on accolades or recognition, or you grew up in abusive homes, or experienced feeling invisible and neglected because of your parent being absent, in some way you may find that these voids, filters, and fillers evolve and our learned coping mechanism is then carried into our adulthood. To feel alive, engaged, accepted, we may choose fillers that aren't healthy. The impact of these unhealthy fillers prevents us from truly surrendering our lives to God. Our attention then shifts to those things and eventually replaces our time with God.

Surrendering requires our time to be well spent with God to keep us blameless and free of those areas. Many of us at times tend to believe that our lives are already surrendered to the Father. However, we forget to give complete control over to God. Giving up control can be one of the hardest things to do in the world, but God must take priority over what we deem as important to us. Our emotions, actions, qualities of life, and ultimately, our destinies are often driven and shaped by our filters, fillers, and voids. God cannot expose these filters, fillers, and voids if you are in denial and unaware of who you really are, but He desires a relationship with you. He wants you to get to a place where you no longer settle, negotiate or compromise bits and pieces of who you are to get your needs met but to where you learn to depend solely on Him. Allow me to challenge you to walk away from that place.

Filters, fillers, and voids are at the core of who we are, the decisions we make, and often are the underlying driving force in our lives. These are at the core of our lives' decisions and belief systems. If our filter is unhealthy or distorted, through the lenses of anxiety, worry, fear, anger, greed, resentment, hatred, competition, jealousy and envy, then our perspective on life changes and makes it difficult for us to surrender fully to God's will in our lives. For instance, living through the abandonment, and neglect through foster care I became fearful of rejection. Unknowingly, I lived my life with walls that pushed away others who had a sincere desire to connect with me. This became the norm for me. When someone actually came along to connect in a more meaningful way, I often kept them at a distance. I was afraid that the same way that I was let down before, abandoned by the ones I trusted the most, was going to happen again. No matter how positive the connection felt or how close we became, that filter remained in the back of my mind and was embedded so deeply within my spirit that connecting with others was made very difficult.

Through the filters of rejection, betrayal, disappointment, and abandonment, my beliefs about relationships were influenced. I felt that those who were closest to me tended to hurt me the most. But as I matriculated through the other stages of my life, I quickly learned that this was a faulty filter. I learned that the more that I viewed my life and the relationships from this filter of what happened in my past, the more it dictated my future. I walked around with a chip on my shoulder, did not trust anyone, and lived in fear of my past. I carried limiting beliefs because of these filters and fillers through statements such as "I can't reveal who I really am because I may get judged…" or, "I don't want to get close to this person because I will eventually get hurt", or, "I'll never be able to trust anyone now since this person betrayed me, or this did not work out before so it probably will never get better." These filters spill into the physical, emotional, mental, spiritual and relational areas of our lives. But if exposed, you will no longer feed into the spirits that eventually intoxicate your mindset through behavioral influences which constrain us in some way as a result of the filters. You will be able to approach these filters with the authority of God's word.

As I surrendered these broken areas of my life, I noticed a change in the way that I thought about them. I began to understand as I surrendered these vulnerable areas to the Father, that the word of God taught me to embrace love always. Regardless of how many times I've been hurt, betrayed, or even mistreated, I began to understand that God was love and that through this love, others will know that I am of Him. The Bible speaks so richly concerning love. *Keep out of debt and owe no man anything, except to love one another; for he who loves his neighbor [who practices loving others] has fulfilled the Law [relating to one's fellowmen, meeting all its requirements]*. (Romans 13:8)

The scripture even says that the most talented individuals are nothing without love. *If I [can] speak in the tongues of men and [even] of angels, but have not love (that reasoning, intentional, spiritual devotion such as is inspired by God's love for and in us), I am only a noisy gong or a clanging cymbal. And if I have prophetic powers (the gift of interpreting the divine will and purpose), and understand all the secret truths and mysteries and possess all knowledge, and if I have [sufficient] faith so that I can remove mountains, but have not love (God's love in me) I am nothing (a useless nobody). Even if I dole out all that I have [to the poor in providing] food, and if I surrender my body to be burned or in order that I may glory, but have not love (God's love in me), I gain nothing*. (1 Cor.13:1-3)

I began to get comfortable with loving others the way God would love them and seeing them through the eyes of God. I adopted a better filter to "love freely and openly as God loves." I even became more open to receiving love from others. It was through the opening of my heart that I attracted the great relationships and friendships that I have today. Other changes in my beliefs concerning the negative situations that arose, helped me learn more about myself and moved me closer to understanding what not to do in those situations.

As you are embarking on this incredible journey of surrendering everything in your life to the will of God, it's important to know that there will be a war in your spirit against doing what you know is right, and what you need to do. You will find that whenever you set your heart on something, there seems to come unexpected opposition from surprising sources. The enemy of our soul endeavors to thwart our spiritual mindset of fighting from a position of moral strength to one bent on mindless victory. You'll come to understand that the spirit which lived within Christ when He died on the cross for our sins, is the same spirit that you have access to once you take on God. But being prepared and ready to take on God's spirit means delving into the spiritual realm. It is within the spiritual realm that the situations we do not see coming are revealed and the spirit of Christ is manifested visibly for others to see the presence of God in us. It is within this realm we also learn to be good stewards of God's presence through fasting, prayer, devotion, and studying His word. In stewarding the presence of God you will find that during the process of trusting fully in Christ, you will be refreshed in a way that allows you to lean into the spiritual ministry and teaching of God the Almighty. You will begin to visualize this new hallowed dominion through the eyes of the spirit which is the light of Christ.

According to Mathew 6:22, " *The eye is the lamp of the body. So if your eye is sound, your entire body will be full of light.*" The eye is of paramount importance in this process of surrendering. It is through the lenses of prayers that focus on the word of God, within the tranquility of spiritual mediation that you will come face-to-face with crucial insights and perspectives, out of which will materialize the presence of God.

When you are not able to see clearly the path set by God's will; when you are blind to the truths that are revealed in His word; when your eyes are closed to His glory and wisdom; your spiritual myopia may be profound but not hopeless. God, in His omnipotence, has the power to transform this wilderness of darkness and loss into unobscured spiritual light. All that is required of you is an unequivocal willingness to begin the process of surrendering everything in your life to His will.

Your vision and purpose in life can often be realized through the power of the Creator. If you are able to conceive, through your mind's spiritual eye, the positive mental imagery of freedom, life, joy, hope and peace, then, without any doubt, these features will manifest themselves in your life over time. It will become easier to seek the truth of heaven. It will be easier for your eyes to see positively what God has in store for you. No matter how broken your situation may be or how insurmountable the opposition, adversity and difficulty which attend you through supreme truth and God's guiding hand, you can grow in ways you never thought imaginable. Most of the time, the God of our salvation will choose us to go through the fire.

NUGGETS OF MOTIVATION TO CARRY YOUR THROUGH

Be willing to go through the fire!

So that [the genuineness] of your faith may be tested, [your faith] which is infinitely more precious than the perishable gold which is tested and purified by fire. [This proving of your faith is intended] to redound to [your] praise and glory and honor when Jesus Christ (the Messiah, the Anointed One) is revealed. (1 Peter 1:7)

What many of us do not recognize when we are experiencing this phenomenon is that going through the fire allows us to become purified, and truly genuine in our ministries, callings, gifting, and purposes. Many of us at the end of our trials become stronger. We experience a heightened sense of awareness and purification that catapults us up to another level of living. You have to be willing to go through the fire. Just as gold is purified through the fire, your faith will allow you to glorify God in a way that fosters spiritual change. The fire of our circumstances, situations, sicknesses, and difficulties begins to transform into being more adept in approaching life from a more mature perspective. We will become stronger in our faith. We must embrace truth even in the midst of circumstances that appear uncomfortable and parched to the point of disintegration. God uses those endeavors to prepare us for our next undertakings; our new insights; our closer walk with Him. God will allow His glory to fall on you in such a way as to teach you more about His character and to have no doubt about who He is. Surrendering unconditionally in the fires to God stimulates an insatiable hunger to grow more and more for Him. In the midst of the fire, you will recognize your true dependence on, and faith in God. His is the sole glory attained in the end. Reflect upon some difficult situations and challenges you managed to overcome in the past year. Can you imagine getting through them without the hand of God attending you? Were you able to spiritually handle all that you struggled through? Did it cause you to pray more? Cry out to God more? Seek more of his presence?

Never get complacent

Growing up in the foster care system can have some damaging effects if you allow it. It is easy to use the pain I endured going through the system and experiencing the negative side of it, nursing the wounds that are left open, but when you surrender, there must be a desire to move forward from glory to glory.

And all of us, as with unveiled face, [because we] continued to behold [in the Word of God] as in a mirror the glory of the Lord, are constantly being transfigured into His very own image in ever increasing splendor and from one degree of glory to another; [for this comes] from the Lord [Who is] the Spirit. (*2Cor 3:18*)

There came a point that I became disgusted when I was around 18 years old. As I was in the process of healing after learning that I would have to find my own way, I was lost and felt very much alone. I needed the wisdom, insight and knowledge to keep me back on the reason why it all began in the first place. Every time I gave into the spirit of God, I was able to experience the fullness of joy that the spirit of God offered. Something in me wanted more. I wanted to be the true example of God's love and I wanted to possess the promises of God. Growing up I loved to sing and have always sung, but even during this period I had no desire to sing. Singing was the thing that got me through every pain and every disappointment. When I lost my desire to sing, I knew that I had allowed all that I'd lived through to get the best of me. As I begin to think about how much time I had invested with others who weren't serious and how much I sacrificed for others, I grew very angry. I thought about all the measures I had gone through to support others and I began to doubt God. But as I recall so vividly, I had gone on a 6-month consecration where I separated myself and began to seek God. I began to understand the quenching and fire that was in me. It was a hunger and thirst to obtain the abundance of the mysteries of God. I began to study until I couldn't study anymore. I wanted to know what I was missing.

When I got into the presence of God, I noticed there was a spirit of complacency that had overtaken my life. The pain and frustration that I felt before me had caused me to stop moving. I stopped growing and desired more. I was stuck. I felt as if the life had left my body and that I was an empty shell and that all that I was and had desired had miscarried inside of me. The more I sat in the presence of God, the more God would begin to show me the promises that He had in store for me, that I would teach and show others the spirit of God. The promise that I would inspire impossibilities. The more I prayed, the more God showed me. The more I dreamed concerning the promise land that I would possess, the more I didn't want to flow in the assignment. I found myself questioning God, asking why?

I began to think about all those that had more than I did, had better circumstances than I did, the support of parents, the support others around them. What I didn't know was that I had something bigger inside of me. My love for God began to inspire me to continue to push. The more I pushed forward despite being the empty vessel that I was, the more I began to see the joy of my salvation, my passion of ministry was restored. I began to chuckle to myself, because the more I got into the things of the Kingdom the more I began to experience the hand of the Lord dealing with my mindset. I came to understand that it was faith and obedience that unlocked the door but it was the anointing that He gives us that enabled me to walk in to action. The spirit of complacency slowly began to change. I began to declare that every gift and talent God gives me, I want to use to fulfil God's desire for my life. I didn't want to miss what God was going to speak.

There are moments in life that we miss simply because we become stuck, or blind to what God is speaking either in our spirits or through others. I began to seek God through much prayer and studying. I found that going a day outside of His presence was a day that I lost in bringing glory and honor to His name. Truthfully, I didn't know how much I really needed to seek God until He began to elevate my level of thinking. The more my thinking changed the more I began to understand. Our potential is only limited by our mindsets and faith in our ability to achieve it.

Although my circumstance wasn't the best, I had faith in knowing that God had my back. I believe that if I hadn't sought God at that moment, and surrendered completely to the Father that I would have delayed my destiny. I didn't want to be like the children of Israel wandering 40 years of my life in the wilderness because they lacked the faith and belief in God. Although they were released from slavery in Egypt under the harsh taskmasters, their mindset was still in bondage. We must not follow their path but be released from the imprisonment in our minds, the mentality that no longer continues to motivate us, the mentality that is stagnated because of the past, or the fear of breaking into the newness that is accessible to the believers daily. God requires more faith and fervency as we move into the Kingdom. Don't become complacent. Though it seems that others around you are moving forward, or prospering, it should not lead to a point of reference for comparing yourself to them. It should be a marker to keep moving despite what comes your way. The beauty in life is that things will be presented to you in every stage. You have the choice to determine how you will respond. I chose to respond with surrendering those moments that I don't even understand fully to the one that created me, and I fully trust that that He will never lead me astray.

Despite life's ups or downs, God promises to be with you. You will find the greatest victories are won through overcoming the things you didn't think you could beat. Why do you think you will not have to go through the valleys to get to your mountain? Why not embrace the opportunity to conquer your weakness? I learned that after asking the question why. I turned that question into WHY NOT? What was it going to hurt by becoming greater? Loving harder? Growing further? Complacency is mere distraction that ultimately leads to losing your purpose in what you were ordained to become. God is waiting for you to catch up and it starts with movement. Action is what will move you towards anything you set your heart and mind to do. What I love about God is that our purpose never changes. God is waiting for us to move forward into all that He has promised for our lives.

Chapter Nine

CROSS YOUR RED SEA

One night while preparing for bed, I began to reflect on my journey. I began to reflect on the brokenness that I felt as a result of the rejection and abandonment I had experienced early in life. I questioned deeply who I was. I remember wrestling with my thoughts as I sat on the edge of my bed. I questioned my purpose. I asked God why did I always get the short end of the stick? Why was I the one used, envied, rejected, cheated, manipulated and left to deal with the struggle of picking up the broken pieces of my life?

It was easy to relive the emotions that were closely attached to the memories of those situations. I lay there feeling distraught and alone. My world had been turned upside down. I felt lost in the myriad of emotions of the moment. I was frustrated. I was angry. I was hurt. In this place of hurt, I fought to close down these thoughts and emotions; to disconnect and find a space where it was just me and Jesus. I willed myself not to feel anything anymore; not to care anymore. The weight of the frustration and anger crushing me was so heavy I didn't have the strength to get up from the edge of my bed. I became so weighed down that I could not sleep, no matter how I tried.

As I continued to wrestle with my thoughts, I soon realized that the burden was too heavy for me to carry. I could no longer make allowances for the mistakes of others. I did not have to strength to carry this burden any longer. In the depth of this struggle, prayer seemed a natural refuge. As I surrendered my spirit to its petition for solace, I felt the warm, slow release of tension deep within my spiritual being. I reprised this experience to highlight one of the paths I seek out for surrendering to the spirit and presence of God. His presence can also permeate every part of your being; the broken; the torn; and the indifferent. God can heal those wounded areas. His healing power will remove the root cause of spiritual malaise. It will calm the raging storms above and beneath the waters of your Red Sea.

The residue of discouragement, bitterness, hatred, lack of forgiveness, and confusion will begin to drip away spiritually and be made naught as a sunrise dissipates the morning dew. God will renew your focus and purpose. You will encounter your season of hope and life. He will revive you again. However, it is your unwavering commitment and staunch determination to cross over the Red Sea in your life that will deliver you to the safe spiritual harbor the living God has promised you.

The biblical account of God's call of Moses, who was used to rescue the Children of Israel out of Egyptian slavery, was prepared by God's spirit to deliver the Children of Israel out of the hands of the Egyptian taskmasters who dealt harshly with them.

Basically, God used Moses to speak directly to Pharaoh to liberate the Children of Israel from Egyptian oppression. To further get the attention of the oppressors, God unleashed 10 plagues. *(Ex.5-12)* Eventually, Pharaoh lets them go, allowing Moses to lead them through the wilderness and across the Red Sea. The Red Sea became dry land and the waters became a wall on both the right and left side. The Egyptians who had begun to go after the Children of Israel with all Pharaoh's horses, chariots and horsemen, were wiped out by the same waters that allowed the Children of Israel to cross over. Then God overthrew the Egyptians in the mist of the Red Sea. *(Ex.14)*

I shared this account because often times the Lord will allow you to face tasks that appear to consume you but when you respond to his missives and admonitions, the power of Christ will be directly manifested to you as will be the keys to your life of freedom. Moses didn't hesitate long enough at the Red Sea for fear to set in, and so God was able to use Moses' hand to deliver those that were in bondage. Often the thing that God wants to free you from is in your reach. Your hands are very powerful. The very gifts, talents, callings and strengths are the things that God will use to enable you to cross over the Red Seas in your life and grant access to the deliverance available to you. God wants you to be liberated from any oppression that you face, whether it's from sin, frustration, broken and unhealthy relationships, or whether you are just living beneath your potential. Why don't you just start looking for the omnipresence of God?

He promises a way of escape. "*For no temptation (no trial regarded as enticing to sin), [no matter how it comes or where it leads] has overtaken you and laid hold on you that is not common to man [that is, no temptation or trial has come to you that is beyond human resistance and that is not adjusted and adapted and belonging to human experience, and such as man can bear]. But God is faithful [to His Word and to His compassionate nature], and He [can be trusted] not to let you be tempted and tried and assayed beyond your ability and strength of resistance and power to endure, but with the temptation He will [always] also provide the way out (the means of escape to a landing place), that you may be capable and strong and powerful to bear up under it patiently.*" *(1 Corinthians 10:13)*

Throughout every moment of surrender to the will and spirit of God, it is of paramount importance that you form a pattern of looking for the presence of God in your situation.

Chapter Ten

CHARGE YOUR ATMOSPERE THROUGH PRAYER

Do not fret or have any anxiety about anything, but in every circumstance and in everything, by prayer and petition (definite requests), with thanksgiving, continue to make your wants known to God. And God's peace [shall be yours, that tranquil state of a soul assured of its salvation through Christ, and so fearing nothing from God and being content with its earthly lot of whatever sort that is, that peace] which transcends all understanding shall garrison and mount guard over your hearts and minds in Christ Jesus. (Philippians 4:6-7)

Spending time in prayer allows us to more fully surrender ourselves to God. Prayer ignites a right spirit in us and opens the door for a more in depth level of intimacy with the Lord. Prayer is a foundational tool that involves God's presence on your journey. When you invoke God's presence in your life, you allow God to circumcise your heart where you are seeking His presence and not His hand. In times where we need to release situations, relationships, and concerns to the Lord, we will be able to experience a release from bondage into a greater realm, spiritually first, then spilling into the natural areas of our lives. Through the Holy Spirit's promptings, you will discover new gifting's, new ministries, new perspectives and insights, and most importantly the instruction for living every moment of your life surrendered to the will and way of the Father. Prayer invokes the heart of God towards action on your behalf. Prayer should remain a daily dialogue between you and God. It builds and secures your relationship in Christ and allows you to access the heavenly realm of handling situations. That's where the strength to let go comes from. Each day on your journey is an opportunity unleash God's power to supernaturally flow throughout your life. It is time to inquire of the Lord for ways to completely surrender your total will to Him.

Key Pieces That Add Spiritual Understanding to Every Moment You Surrender

Key 1: Admitting that you have a problem and seeking help from God are the most important keys in the process. Remain transparent. When we are honest, God can circumcise our hearts in truth and righteousness. *"You will know the Truth, and the Truth will set you free." (John 8:32)*

Key 2: Set a time/place - This is critical for you as you surrender every moment of your life to God. Establish a place to seek Him and pray to Him. This can be in your car, on your lunch break, before bed, early in the morning or even during worship at a local church. Choose a place that is easily accessible where you meet with God. Make a daily decision to release it to God in much prayer and through fasting. This means that in all humility and a humble heart share your vulnerability. This process will give you the courage to look outside of yourself for comfort, direction, grace and strength to overcome areas of weakness.

Key 3: Expect a Fresh Anointing - Prayer unlocks mysteries, ministries, and unfolds His will for you. Prayer can allow you to draw on God's strength, thoughts towards us, peace, and patience as we release things to Him. It is the anointing that enables you to accomplish all that you are called to do. Remain accountable for your spiritual growth in prayer. Continuously examine yourself to ensure that you are allowing God's way and will to be done in your life. This comes with consistent focus through prayer and time in the presence of God. Your accountability will push you for a deeper level of knowledge of His will and motivate you with His power to carry that out. This key unlocks the supernatural power of God. Prayer unleashes the authority of God in your life. There are things that God wants to supernaturally reveal to you, to speak directly to your spirit and heart. There are things that He wants to secure in you as you surrender. Faith and the spirit of the Lord will be able to build you in areas that you consider weak, impossible to resolve, or broken. *"We are assured and know that all things work together and are [fitting into a plan] for good to and for those who love God and are called according to [His] design and purpose." (Romans 8:28)* What the enemy thought was going to break you, destroy you, God will use that very thing to bless you and increase your faith in Him. He will reveal things that flesh and blood cannot reveal and you will see Him. When you surrender the most difficult situations to Him, and take your hands off of it, then God can fully show up! You will not be disappointed!

Chapter Eleven

THE WORD OF GOD ACTIVATES THE SPIRIT OF GOD IN YOU

For this is the covenant that I will make with the house of Israel after those days, says the Lord: I will imprint My laws upon their minds, even upon their innermost thoughts and understanding, and engrave them upon their hearts; and I will be their God, and they shall be My people. (Hebrews 8:10)

The Bible is one of the oldest books in the world, yet it is still living, powerful and active in the life of the believers. When you open the Bible, ask God to speak to you about the words on those pages, the parables that are written, and the interpretation of certain words. God honors His word. If you are spending time in His word, He will begin to show you more of who He is. On your journey you will discover more mysteries that will change how you approach life and His will for you. You will gain more wisdom, begin to lead a life of faith and increase God's presence in every situation. The word of God will begin to be your daily substance. As you surrender to God, you will find that the biblical principles outlined in the Bible, will connect you to all of the promises God has for your life. How can you obtain the promises of God when you don't know them? You have to know what God says about situations before you can believe them.

The word is an illumination of what heaven knows but until you open the pages, you will not know. You will begin to see the dimension of God in those areas when you are in the present moment pursuing time well spent in the word of God. I came to understand that without the word of God I was operating in a realm of limitations.

My eyes were closed to other solutions, approaches and alternatives. But, your miracles will require knowing the word of God. Knowing what God says about certain situations gives you the assurance of your faith and enables you to live a life of obedience. God understands the value to you of knowing His word and that this knowing can penetrate your relationship that breeds more of His insight and mysteries of the Gospel. He wants those words to leap off the pages into your spirit so that you can be able to see Him in every situation in your life. The word of God is so powerful in what it does to your faith. He has given you free access to His knowledge, miracles, and much more. Learn to take God at His word. Here are some scriptures that speaks on how powerful the word of God is.

BIBLE VERSES ABOUT THE WORD OF GOD

Deuteronomy 8:3

And He humbled you and allowed you to hunger and fed you with manna, which you did not know nor did your fathers know, that He might make you recognize and personally know that man does not live by bread only, but man lives by every word that proceeds out of the mouth of the Lord.

Psalm 119:9

How shall a young man cleanse his way? By taking heed and keeping watch [on himself] according to Your word [conforming his life to it].

Isaiah 40:8

The grass withers, the flower fades, but the word of our God will stand forever.

Matthew 24:35

Sky and earth will pass away, but My words will not pass away.

Matthew 4:4

But He replied, It has been written, Man shall not live and be upheld and sustained by bread alone, but by every word that comes forth from the mouth of God.

Luke 11:28

But He said, Blessed (happy and to be envied) rather are those who hear the Word of God and obey and practice it!

Philippians 2:14-16

Do all things without grumbling and faultfinding and complaining [against God] and questioning and doubting [among yourselves], That you may show yourselves to be blameless and guileless, innocent and uncontaminated, children of God without blemish (faultless, unrebukable) in the midst of a crooked and wicked generation [spiritually perverted and perverse], among whom you are seen as bright lights (stars or beacons shining out clearly) in the [dark] world, Holding out [to it] and offering [to all men] the Word of Life, so that in the day of Christ I may have something of which exultantly to rejoice and glory in that I did not run my race in vain or spend my labor to no purpose.

John 1:14

And the Word (Christ) became flesh (human, incarnate) and tabernacled (fixed His tent of flesh, lived awhile) among us; and we [actually] saw His glory (His honor, His majesty), such glory as an only begotten son receives from his father, full of grace (favor, loving-kindness) and truth.

John 7:38

He who believes in Me [who cleaves to and trusts in and relies on Me] as the Scripture has said, From his innermost being shall flow [continuously] springs and rivers of living water.

John 8:31-32

So Jesus said to those Jews who had believed in Him, If you abide in My word [hold fast to My teachings and live in accordance with them], you are truly My disciples. And you will know the Truth, and the Truth will set you free.

Hebrews 1:3-4

He is the sole expression of the glory of God [the Light-being, the out-raying or radiance of the divine], and He is the perfect imprint and very image of [God's] nature, upholding and maintaining and guiding and propelling the universe by His mighty word of power. When He had by offering Himself accomplished our cleansing of sins and riddance of guilt, He sat down at the right hand of the divine Majesty on high, [Taking a place and rank by which] He Himself became as much superior to angels as the glorious Name (title) which He has inherited is different from and more excellent than theirs.

Hebrews 4:12

For the Word that God speaks is alive and full of power [making it active, operative, energizing, and effective]; it is sharper than any two-edged sword, penetrating to the dividing line of the breath of life (soul) and [the immortal] spirit, and of joints and marrow [of the deepest parts of our nature], exposing and sifting and analyzing and judging the very thoughts and purposes of the heart.

James 1:21-22

So get rid of all uncleanness and the rampant outgrowth of wickedness, and in a humble (gentle, modest) spirit receive and welcome the Word which implanted and rooted [in your hearts] contains the power to save your souls.But be doers of the Word [obey the message], and not merely listeners to it, betraying yourselves [into deception by reasoning contrary to the Truth].

2 Timothy 3:16-17

Every Scripture is God-breathed (given by His inspiration) and profitable for instruction, for reproof and conviction of sin, for correction of error and discipline in obedience, [and] for training in righteousness (in holy living, in conformity to God's will in thought, purpose, and action), So that the man of God may be complete and proficient, well fitted and thoroughly equipped for every good work.

Chapter Twelve

PERSONAL BATTLEGROUNDS DRAW US TO GOD'S VICTORY

Yet amid all these things we are more than conquerors [a]and gain a surpassing victory through Him Who loved us. (Romans 8:37)

God, when we surrender to Him, is calling us out of a certain spirit or situations. Often we are in battles that those around us may not realize we are in. Personal battlegrounds are ways that we as believers truly come to knowledge of the characteristics and nature of Christ. God uses those situations to draw us closer to Him, to test our faith and to take on the compatibility of His will in our lives. Personal battlegrounds can be the places where we experience God's victory the most. We tend to be surprised, shocked, confused, and distracted in the battle rather than standing still to see the power of God.

Coming into this season remember through all of your opposition, adversity, hurts, and moments of battle in secret, you will find the ingredients to God's victory and success. Instead of finding those situations irritating, frustrating, or causes to become engulfed, know that the battle is always won before you go into it.

For I know the thoughts and plans that I have for you, says the Lord, thoughts and plans for welfare and peace and not for evil, to give you hope in your final outcome. (Jer.29:11)

If in the thick of your personal battleground you decide to give into your emotions, you will eventually become a byproduct of that battle. You will succumb to the enemy's tactics, and traps. You will become so engulfed that you lose sight of the position of victory that you already have through Christ. A nugget that God revealed to me was that despite all of the fears, frustrations, and concerns, I was not operating in faith. I was operating in a mode of limitations. It is impossible to walk in faith when you are fearful. When you get wrapped up into the emotion of things, often times you become irrational.

I remember many days that I wrestled within myself to continue to line up with all that God was calling me to do. One night I had left a powerful meeting. I was driving alone and just singing softly to the worship music that was playing in my car. I began to go into prayer concerning the areas that I was wrestling in. Often times in my car or when I rode with others, I would go in to a silent prayer for guidance mainly as I transitioned into adulthood. I was dealing with a lot concerning my situation with both my parents re-entering my life. How I was going to allow them back in my life after years of not being actively involved? I began to think about how my situation forced me to become independent, forced me to think larger, and pushed me into seeking God like never before. I began to get overwhelmed as I evaluated the number of individuals that had ever dealt with anything remotely like this in my circle and I came to find that at that time it was just my twin sister. I began to see that my reality was do or die spiritually. It was give in to the plan God had for my life or follow my emotions. I began to notice that the more I prayed, the more I wrestled. Within myself I had to come to grips with all that I had suffered as a result of the decisions of my parents. What I came to find is that I wasn't ready to lose the anger and resentment that I felt. I wasn't ready to fully comprehend the magnitude of what was happening. There was no doubt that my history would ever connect me to my ministry, however, there was something unfamiliar with this particular wrestle. I wanted more of God's presence. I wanted more faith and strength to stand up to the challenges that were before me. There was a part of God's plan that I didn't know nor would ever be privy to. I began to see my life and all of the unexpected turns, all of the disappointments, and broken relationships that shattered my world. I began to question if God had only stepped in, these relationships would not have died. My family wouldn't have been separated.

Perhaps you may be thinking the same thing. But what I want to share with you is that there is no better timing then the Lord's timing. There is purpose to your delay. Just as Jesus showed up and called Lazarus in John, Chapter 11, from the grave after he died, some things in you must die before God can call you forth.

Some situations have to die and fall apart for God to get your attention that something needs to be completed in this season.

In John 11:4, when Lazarus was sick and his sisters Mary and Martha wanted to Jesus to come, His reply was, "*This sickness is not to end in death; but [on the contrary] it is to honor God and to promote His glory, that the Son of God may be glorified through (by) it.*" There are situations that God uses that will bring glory to the Kingdom of Christ. It may feel as if you've been forsaken but the purpose in your delay is to believe God for the impossible in your situation. He uses our situations to strengthen our faith just as he did with Martha and Mary.

Isn't that like what we do when we don't see the manifestations of what we've prayed about, fasted about and had faith to accomplish? We find ourselves stuck on what didn't happen or work out for us. We miss out on instructions that are pivotal for our success because we take a sabbatical in the presence of God when situations unexpectedly take a turn in a direction that isn't what we ever thought we would face. We stop seeking the face of God to declare that it is a waste, and we lose our zeal for the things of God. But when you surrender those things to the Lord, you will be given the grace and mercy to trust Him in the midst of the pain. Now is the time to take a closer look at where you left your goals, dreams, and desires. Did you abort them with your lack of faith? Did you lose time in the present by focusing on what happened to you in the past? Or did you slowly walk away from it because it did not manifest in the time that you wanted? Or have you just forgotten and lost track of where you left those things because you didn't think God would ever show up?

The Bible says in Proverbs 13:12, "*Hope deferred makes the heart sick, but when the desire is fulfilled, it is a tree of life*." You lose hope, you become sick, you become deficient in your ability to move freely into the place God has for you because you are not at your best. You begin to silently carry dead weight that when you begin to move forward, pulls you back and weighs you down. It limits your ability to operate at your full potential because you begin to over work yourself as a result of the weight you are carrying. When you lose hope, it filters into every aspect of our lives and creates distractions, loss of joy, and loss of motivation and zeal. You become blind to the root cause of the sickness because it is beneath the surface, and has grown to be such a part of who we are that we begin to naturally claim the sickness as who we are. We've become so connected to it that we lose sight of who we are and what God has for us. That is why we must stay in the presence of God, and continually examine ourselves to see the blemishes in our armor. The things we wrestle with are because we are in the spiritual warfare of entering into another realm. However, you become a double threat when you stay in the presence long enough for God to reveal Himself to you and the sources of the sicknesses that you carry. The thing that I love the most about God is that He knows every last one of us, and where we are. He will meet you right there in the middle of your divorce, the middle of your diagnosis, the middle of your job situations, the middle of your marriage, in the middle of your loss and provide your source of comfort and strength. He knows your beginning and your end, and when you fully surrender every moment to him, you take the spirit of Christ to every place of hurt, pain, or destruction and He will free you.

The light of his glory will begin to illuminate more of your areas with His glory so that others may be encouraged and strengthened. It is not enough for you to just cry it out or to take Him to each area, but God will require you to let go of the negatives and find the good in your situation, even if it means facing the truth or dealing with a difficult situation. We often times will go through our lives not recognizing that we have buried our issues for so long that it becomes familiar to us. It isn't until we surrender to the will of God in every moment that we begin to see the right estimate of who we are. It's your time to be released from *the burial wrappings*! Nothing should hold us back from reaching our true potential.

In John 11: 43-44, *When He had said this, He shouted with a loud voice, Lazarus, come out! And out walked the man who had been dead, his hands and feet wrapped in burial cloths (linen strips), and with a [burial] napkin bound around his face. Jesus said to them, Free him of the burial wrappings and let him go.*

Now is the time for me to call you forth and out by the power of God in me. Just as in John 11:43 when Jesus shouted in a loud voice, "*Lazarus, come out*!" the Bible declares that this man came out and was still bound up in his grave clothes. Jesus began to call him forward in the liberty that he pre-ordained. It isn't enough for God to call you forward, but he will release you from everything that is binding your mobility, your stewardship, your zeal, your family, relationships and destiny. He will give you the ability to walk in the authority and liberty. Every dead situation or limited mindset must let you go and anything that you are held captive to. This is essentially one of the most powerful ways that God moves you forward and accelerates your growth. The moment that you surrender, you are loosed to walk into the liberty of Christ.

After I let go of the things that held me captive, I refused to live in the shell of bitterness, hopelessness, negativity and resentment. I decided that I would never look back unless it was to testify of the power of God. You can now love the skin you are in, live in freedom, and walk confidently into your purpose. You can now let go of procrastinating, of the addictions, and build and establish healthy relationships that support your change. Your situation has to release you to carry the fruit of spiritual health and joy. It has to release you to operate in the realm of God's power that reveals His glory and works in our lives.

Chapter Thirteen

FEAR PARALYZES YOUR FAITH BUT FAITH PARALYZES YOUR FEAR!

Fear not [there is nothing to fear], for I am with you; do not look around you in terror and be dismayed, for I am your God. I will strengthen and harden you to difficulties, yes, I will help you; yes, I will hold you up and retain you with My [victorious] right hand of rightness and justice. (Isaiah 41:10)

When you operate through the faith in God, He will save you. He will groom and prosper you while you are in the battle. Don't sit there long enough for fear to set in, for emotions to swallow you in the belly of that whale! All of the pressure and attacks are intended to distract you from the victory that you already have. God knew all that you were going to go through and have been through. He knows everything you prayed about, everything you cried about, everything you wrestled with. You can trust and believe He has use of you.

Now is the time to refocus your mindset knowing that God has your back. Personal battlegrounds strengthen you and releases the power of God on you to come out of the battle in total victory. You will begin to see that God's hand is upon you and despite the opposition, and the things that were thrown your way in the battle of the enemy, you will know that God was carrying you. "*But no weapon that is formed against you shall prosper, and every tongue that shall rise against you in judgment you shall show to be in the wrong. This [peace, righteousness, security, triumph over opposition] is the heritage of the servants of the Lord [those in whom the ideal Servant of the Lord is reproduced]; this is the righteousness or the vindication which they obtain from Me [this is that which I impart to them as their justification], says the Lord.* (*Isaiah.54:17*)

To meet every blow that the enemy has at your life, your ordained purpose, you don't have to dribble too much before you shoot. In the end, when it comes down to it, the enemy will jump ship the moment you begin to speak the faith. When you begin to declare the word of God as your final authority, and pray intentionally for God's presence to manifest, you will paralyze fear. Fear will leave you and your faith will make you whole, courageous, daring, and will open the door for your faith to be increased. Faith will compel you to a firm space of grace on the grounds of victory. Faith will reveal things in you that fear didn't want you to get together, discover, and appreciate!

Chapter 14

COMMEMORATE YOUR WILDERNESS

The greatest miracles and power of God are seen in your wilderness experiences. It prepares you for your greatest miracles. The wilderness experiences are the breakdown experiences through which we tend to find ourselves, find God, and become humbled on the right estimate of who you are in the sight of God. I can honestly say that the times when my life was broken in pieces, when I experienced the shackles of principalities in certain areas of my life, doubt, hurt, rejections, abandonment, fears, I remembered how my eyes were opened to the things that really matter in my walk with God. The moment that happened the rest was history. It was the place of miracles, the place where I met God. When I was at the crossroads of forgiveness, and disturbed with individuals who caused me distress as well as those who walked out of my life, I began to experience God's provision in a way that restored my vision! No longer did I live in the past of the situations that I experienced. No longer did I want to recount the words that were spoken. No longer did I want to be discouraged in ministry and serving. No longer did I want to kick against what God was doing in my life. I began to remember all of the countless lives that I was able to minister to. I began to remember the fire of God that started when I moved to Maryland. I remember one of my first jobs in high school was working for McDonalds and making $6.80 per hour. I remember walking to work and when I got off late, walking home at night. That was one of the darkest seasons of my life. There were times I was working in the drive-through and people would ask me why was I so happy. I'd always say the power of God is changing my life. They didn't know who I was or what my purpose was but one thing they knew was that the light of God was in me and that I would not be there for long.

I had an encounter with an older woman who saw me at the front cash register as I was working. She came in as if she had just gotten off of the street and alcohol was on her breath. She began to speak a word to me. Initially, I was confused because for one, she had been on the street and secondly, for her to stop me and give me a word that she said she heard in her heart touched me. I began to shed a few tears at this woman's humility. Then the words that preceded out of her mouth were, "Don't carry the hurt of others for too long, daughter. Give it to God and He will watch over you." She said, "I don't care what you go through always smile." She showed me the wrinkles around her mouth. She said despite her bad decisions and mistakes that God had graced her to have joy on the inside and that she would live for Him whether she was on the street or not. Immediately, I wanted to give her all that I had but I didn't have anything. She went on to say that God is going to bless you in ways you will never imagine. She said, "Forgive, daughter."

I recount this story because even in her vulnerability, she touched my heart with love and compassion. I began to feel the presence of God come over me. I began to cry one tear at a time and I decided that I will always stay in the state of receiving all that God intends for me, regardless of what it appeared to be and regardless of the messenger.

That was one of my greatest miracles, not because I was working, not because I had somewhere to stay, but because God met me and used someone to bless me spiritually. His words through her were life to me. I was at my lowest level working there. I was humiliated because while everyone else enjoy having things given to them I had to work. I couldn't even afford to pay for my senior pictures. It activated a new level of thinking in me. That day at the register in McDonalds. I began to see life in a new way and embraced the fact that all though I was working at McDonalds, He was using this to attract me to His purpose and will for my life.

I didn't just limit God to speak to me in the four walls of the church but I wanted God everywhere I was. I wanted Him to show up. Throughout my life, God has sent individuals who were angels at critical points in my life. I began to think back on those events when I was at my lowest point; when I literally felt like I was nothing and had nothing. Even then I celebrated all that He did. All though I was in my wilderness most of my youth, I saw the faithfulness of God even when I wasn't faithful. Likened to the

Children of Israel, I placed situations, habits, other things as a God. I prioritized and got distracted by the cares of this life and yet and still God still carried me. He blessed me in His grace to make it through each of those situations with greater levels of insight and a different mindset towards small beginnings. To this day, I love doing small things. I appreciate the small things of doing someone's hair or giving a seed, or card of appreciation. Big things often start small. Big miracles often start at the most vulnerable, sensitive point of our lives. The lowest parts of us, the darkest parts of us, begin to see a glimpse of what God is doing and catches fire on the inside. The fire of God inside of us begins to speak to us, fill us up, and mold and shape us in to the child of God we are ordained to be. It begins to strengthen us to let go of the things that pose the greatest risks, distractions, and demises.

I shared this because I want you to look back on some times when you were in a low place; when you were grieving the loss of certain things; when you experienced hurt of some sort. Look back and think about how you made it through. Remember the things that God brought you out of and understand that it was in the wilderness that you first saw God work something out for you. It was when you were jobless, and now you have a job. When you were alone, he sent your spouse or friendships. When you were sick, mentally and physically, He healed you. When you were enslaved to your addictions and habits, He freed you. Begin to commemorate your wilderness.

Thank God for those things that happened because they stretched and forced you to be intentional with allowing God into those areas. You had the privilege to be brought into some things that were for the best. You with your own eyes witnessed a miracle unfold, and the level of excellence and strength that you now have was a result. Most importantly it cultivated a relationship with Christ that equips and prepares you for each season of your life.

BEGIN TO REJOICE

The wilderness will chip away the old character and birth a new promise in you. Through the wilderness you will discover the implanted sense of purpose that God has for you. You will begin to experience the fresh anointing that God has available to you. His spirit will never run dry in you. Through His presence in every part of you and your life, you will come alive. I declare an outpouring of the power and spirit of God right now.

GET INTENTIONAL

Surrendering to God is all about activating your spirit to align with the light of Christ. You should live to worship God for whatever process He is taking you through. Lose yourself in Christ. This part of the surrendering process is a decision to strengthen your identity in Christ. Your life is hidden in Christ and the power of God will strengthen, change your focus, and turn your heart to God.

Jude 20: 20-24 tells us:

But you, beloved, build yourselves up [founded] on your most holy faith [make progress, rise like an edifice higher and higher], praying in the Holy Spirit; Guard and keep yourselves in the love of God; expect and patiently wait for the mercy of our Lord Jesus Christ (the Messiah)—[which will bring you] unto life eternal. And refute [so as to] convict some who dispute with you, and on some have mercy who waver and doubt. [Strive to] save others, snatching [them] out of [the] fire; on others take pity [but] with fear, loathing even the garment spotted by the flesh and polluted by their sensuality. Now to Him Who is able to keep you without stumbling or slipping or falling, and to present [you] unblemished (blameless and faultless) before the presence of His glory in triumphant joy and exultation [with unspeakable, ecstatic delight] ....

Through prayer every disorder, every label, and any damage can be reversed for you. The enemy of our souls wants us to block the inception of the spirit of God in us, wants to silence the praise and worship in our lives, wants to hinder our spirit that was designed to worship Him and form us as image bearers of Him. The enemy wants to use real things, situations, and circumstances to occupy our mind and form strongholds. By connecting to the spiritual mind of Christ you will begin to hear, on another level, what the spirit has to say to you. You will hear the sound of revival in your heart and mind. You will begin to be led by the Spirit and experience the unfolding of the power of God when you need it most. His glory will illuminate you, and allow you to experience the patience and process that creates a greater level of hunger and thirsting after righteousness. It will create a new level of excellence. Be willing to wait for God in every situation because surrendering allows you to sense the change and glory of God in you.

Learn to commemorate the wilderness experiences because you are being conformed to the image of Christ. In the wilderness, God will begin to humble you and speak to you in those places that you feel hope is scarce, when you feel God is unresponsive, and when you feel most isolated, vulnerable, lost and even attacked. In every moment of surrender there will be times when you will doubt yourself, feel alienated, struggle the most, but God will begin to breathe on you to show His glory to you. The wilderness is the spiritual path that God takes His people to focus and solely depend on Him. You will find that the greater the purpose on your life, the longer the wilderness experience will be, because God can prepare and equip you for the life He destined you to have. In the wilderness, God begins to inspire you with His promise.

In my wilderness, I experienced depression and traumatic life experiences. At times I felt stagnated and frustrated with the process. I didn't want to go through the suffering. The wilderness will build and allow us to become a man or woman after God's own heart. The wilderness is not because God does not love you, but because He is preparing, testing and developing your character. HOWEVER, don't despise this place, because your promises are connected with your period of testing. God uses the wilderness to invest in us His seed of promise, His purpose, His spirit and conviction of our faith. His hope and comfort makes all things new and He begins to push us into another realm of following Him forward. It forces the believer to become privy and sensitive to the leading of God. The wilderness makes you God's example and miracle to the world. He will use you to be a light for others in dark situations, to manifest his glory. When you get out of your wilderness, you will be the one to showcase the glory of God. The wilderness births in you an ability to embrace the miracle working power of our God. It's in the wilderness that you change forever in God's glory. You will never be the same. You are changed forever and when you live out your life and the promises of God, you will be full of the faith to move mountains, overcome giants, and live with the weight of God's glory on your life. The wilderness changes you from the inside out. Everything that you are waiting for in the wilderness is right there in the glory of God.

Chapter Fifteen

WITHOUT EXPECTANCY, THERE IS NO RELEASE

You will guard him and keep him in perfect and constant peace whose mind [both its inclination and its character] is stayed on You, because he commits himself to You, leans on You, and hopes confidently in You. (*Isaiah 26:3)*

Train your spirit to connect with the spirit of God. If there is no connection, there will not be a spirit of expectancy to change. Expectancy in the believer's life is a fragrance of faith, trust, and hope in the spiritual realm. *Be strong and let your heart take courage, all you who wait for and hope for and expect the Lord!* (Psalm 31:24) There is a realm that God wants you to usher in His glory, effecting change in the Earth so the glory of God begins to transform. You must be willing to let all the negatives in your life go in exchange for His deep infusion of His presence, knowledge and wisdom in your life. Your answer lies in entering the "*Secret Place*."

Psalm 91:1 says, "*He who dwells in the secret place of the Most High shall remain stable and fixed under the shadow of the Almighty [Whose power no foe can withstand]*."

The "*Secret Place*" is where the invasion of the Holy Spirit overcomes the area of difficulty. The power of expectancy can assist you in surrendering fully to the will of God. When the mantle switches in your spiritual realm, you will have expectancy that allows you to anticipate the moving and healing of God in your relationships, friendships, and heart. You will experience the breaking of yokes of bondage. God wants to do something greater than what you thought was ever possible.

But those who wait for the Lord [who expect, look for, and hope in Him] shall change and renew their strength and power; they shall lift their wings and mount up [close to God] as eagles [mount up to the sun]; they shall run and not be weary, they shall walk and not faint or become tired. (Isaiah 40:31)

Chapter Sixteen

CHANGE YOUR INNER CIRCLE!

He who walks [as a companion] with wise men will be wise,
But the companions of [conceited, dull-witted] fools [are fools themselves and] will experience harm. (Proverbs 13:20)

As you journey through your life, it's important to be careful who you have in your circle. I was in a place that I was walking around dead. I needed to be alive again. I needed to be rejuvenated. I needed an authentic sound and needed to be connected to others who are the spirit realm. I was an empty shell. But as I surrendered my life to the spirit of Christ, it shifted me to another dimension. I wanted something more. I wanted to see a shift in the things in my life to come together. I found that those who walked out of my life, did me the greatest favor I could ever want. Changing your inner circle is powerful and will be the biggest influence to your spiritual journey. You want to center yourself with others more spiritually mature and stronger than you. Don't be afraid to take a risk and eliminate the fear of meeting your destiny. Relationships are integral to your foundation spiritually.

Prayer of Surrender

God, I confess that I am a work in progress. I do not have it all together and I am at a place in my life where I need to release the things that have left me broken, lost and angry. I have lived a life of silence and have held on to things that I can't change. Now it's time to leave these things at your feet, as you know what to do with them. It's time for me to live the life I have desired of freedom, and strength to face tomorrow, and that my joy would remain. I give this to you__________, and desire to never pick it back up. I rely on you to take care of all of the broken pieces of my life that are before you in this moment of prayer and that you would bring healing. I am now willing to release these things to you, and trust you for my next steps.

I am ready to embrace the NOW moments by forgetting the past, living in the present and looking forward with expectancy to the future. I pray for your wisdom and guidance on how to deal with the daily compromises, worries and distractions of life and pray you would strengthen me to react to life's situations with a Godly response. In doing this I am completely relying on you and resting in the hope that you have made available to all. I am believing you for beauty for my ashes, and that you would remove the spirit of heaviness, break every generational curse, and remove all strongholds in my life. I pray for strength to let go and the faith in your plan for my life.

I repent for the times when I have allowed judgmental attitudes and negativity to rule me and to cause me to respond in a way contrary to your word. Show me how to remember your mercy toward me so that I can extend your mercy to others, and remove any root of bitterness. Humble me in areas where I think I have it all together and show me how to restore others in a spirit of meekness. I pray that you would show me how to love and forgive others as you have loved and forgiven me.

Lord, I come to you and pray for growth in grace, expressed in patience, meekness, and love. Lord, I desire to keep the commandments of our Master and follow His example. I realize that it is my reasonable service to Him and the only worthy evidence of our gratitude for all that He has done. Help me to remain in unceasing prayer and to examine and correct any motives contrary to your word. I realize that motives are made manifest in the blessings they bring. Create in me a clean heart and renew in me a right spirit. Lastly, I release my entire life and will, my body, heart, and mind, every talent, gift, and idea to you that you may make me whole, have your way in my life, and forever get the glory. In Jesus' name. Amen.

SCRIPTURES TO READ, CONFESS AND PRAY

Now is the time to go deeper with God and to rediscover our inner strength, experience his perfection, and allow His will to be done. Surrendering on your journey will expose hidden treasures that uncover the unshakable and uplifting power of healing and freedom birthed through the power of release!!

Here are a few scriptures to meditate on that will get you started as you seek God in every moment of your surrender:

Psalm 1:1-3

BLESSED (HAPPY, fortunate, prosperous, and enviable) is the man who walks and lives not in the counsel of the ungodly [following their advice, their plans and purposes], nor stands [submissive and inactive] in the path where sinners walk, nor sits down [to relax and rest] where the scornful [and the mockers] gather.But his delight and desire are in the law of the Lord, and on His law (the precepts, the instructions, the teachings of God) he habitually meditates (ponders and studies) by day and by night. And he shall be like a tree firmly planted [and tended] by the streams of water, ready to bring forth its fruit in its season; its leaf also shall not fade or wither; and everything he does shall prosper [and come to maturity].

Psalm 18:30

As for God, His way is perfect! The word of the Lord is tested and tried; He is a shield to all those who take refuge and put their trust in Him.

Psalm 25:9-14

He leads the humble in what is right, and the humble He teaches His way. All the paths of the Lord are mercy and steadfast love, even truth and faithfulness are they for those who keep His covenant and His testimonies. For Your name's sake, O Lord, pardon my iniquity and my guilt, for [they are] great. Who is the man who reverently fears and worships the Lord? Him shall He teach in the way that he should choose. He himself shall dwell at ease, and his offspring shall inherit the land. The secret [of the sweet, satisfying companionship] of the Lord have they who fear (revere and worship) Him, and He will show them His covenant and reveal to them its [deep, inner] meaning.

Psalm 29:11

The Lord will give [unyielding and impenetrable] strength to His people; the Lord will bless His people with peace.

Psalm 31:24

Be strong and let your heart take courage, all you who wait for and hope for and expect the Lord!

Psalm 55:22

Cast your burden on the Lord [releasing the weight of it] and He will sustain you; He will never allow the [consistently] righteous to be moved (made to slip, fall, or fail).

Psalm 62:7-8

With God rests my salvation and my glory; He is my Rock of unyielding strength and impenetrable hardness, and my refuge is in God! Trust in, lean on, rely on, and have confidence in Him at all times, you people; pour out your hearts before Him. God is a refuge for us (a fortress and a high tower). Selah [pause, and calmly think of that]!

Psalm 86:2

Preserve my life, for I am godly and dedicated; O my God, save Your servant, for I trust in You [leaning and believing on You, committing all and confidently looking to You, without fear or doubt].

Psalm 86:5

For You, O Lord, are good, and ready to forgive [our trespasses, sending them away, letting them go completely and forever]; and You are abundant in mercy and loving-kindness to all those who call upon You.

Psalm 86:7

In the day of my trouble.
I will call on You, for You will answer me.

Psalm 97:10

O you who love the Lord, hate evil; He preserves the lives of His saints (the children of God), He delivers them out of the hand of the wicked.

1 Peter 5:7

Casting the whole of your care [all your anxieties, all your worries, all your concerns, once and for all] on Him, for He cares for you affectionately and cares about you watchfully.

2 Peter 1:3

For His divine power has bestowed upon us all things that [are requisite and suited] to life and godliness, through the [full, personal] knowledge of Him Who called us by and to His own glory and excellence (virtue).

Matthew 6:33

But seek (aim at and strive after) first of all His kingdom and His righteousness (His way of doing and being right), and then all these things taken together will be given you besides.

Matthew 11:27-29

All things have been entrusted *and* delivered to Me by My Father; and no one fully knows *and* accurately understands the Son except the Father, and no one fully knows *and* accurately understands the Father except the Son and anyone to whom the Son deliberately wills to make Him known. Come to Me, all you who labor and are heavy-laden *and* overburdened, and I will cause you to rest. [I will ease and relieve and refresh your souls.] Take My yoke upon you and learn of Me, for I am gentle (meek) and humble (lowly) in heart, and you will find rest (relief and ease and refreshment and recreation and blessed quiet) for your souls.

Matthew 16:19

I will give you the keys of the kingdom of heaven; and whatever you bind (declare to be improper and unlawful) on earth must be what is already bound in heaven; and whatever you loose (declare lawful) on earth must be what is already loosed in heaven.

Matthew 16:26

For what will it profit a man if he gains the whole world and forfeits his life [his blessed life in the kingdom of God]? Or what would a man give as an exchange for his [blessed] life [in the kingdom of God]?

Matthew 22:37

And He replied to him, You shall love the Lord your God with all your heart and with all your soul and with all your mind (intellect).

Mark 4:24

And He said to them, Be careful what you are hearing. The measure [of thought and study] you give [to the truth you hear] will be the measure [of virtue and knowledge] that comes back to you—and more [besides] will be given to you who hear.

Luke 9:23

And He said to all, If any person wills to come after Me, let him deny himself [disown himself, forget, lose sight of himself and his own interests, refuse and give up himself] and take up his cross daily and follow Me [cleave steadfastly to Me, conform wholly to My example in living and, if need be, in dying also].

John 6:51

I [Myself] am this Living Bread that came down from heaven. If anyone eats of this Bread, he will live forever; and also the Bread that I shall give for the life of the world is My flesh (body).

John 7:17

If any man desires to do His will (God's pleasure), he will know (have the needed illumination to recognize, and can tell for himself) whether the teaching is from God or whether I am speaking from Myself and of My own accord and on My own authority.

John 15:15

I do not call you servants (slaves) any longer, for the servant does not know what his master is doing (working out). But I have called you My friends, because I have made known to you everything that

I have heard from My Father. [I have revealed to you everything that I have learned from Him.]

1 John 1:9

If we [freely] admit that we have sinned and confess our sins, He is faithful and just (true to His own nature and promises) and will forgive our sins [dismiss our lawlessness] and [continuously] cleanse us from all unrighteousness [everything not in conformity to His will in purpose, thought, and action].

Joshua 1:9

Have not I commanded you? Be strong, vigorous, and very courageous. Be not afraid, neither be dismayed, for the Lord your God is with you wherever you go.

Isaiah 22:22

And the key of the house of David I will lay upon his shoulder; he shall open and no one shall shut, he shall shut and no one shall open.

Isaiah 40:28

Have you not known? Have you not heard? The everlasting God, the Lord, the Creator of the ends of the earth, does not faint or grow weary; there is no searching of His understanding.

Isaiah 41:10

Fear not [there is nothing to fear], for I am with you; do not look around you in terror and be dismayed, for I am your God. I will strengthen and harden you to difficulties, yes, I will help you; yes, I will hold you up and retain you with My [victorious] right hand of rightness and justice.

Jeremiah 6:16

Thus says the Lord: Stand by the roads and look; and ask for the eternal paths, where the good, old way is; then walk in it, and you will find rest for your souls. But they said, We will not walk in it!

Jeremiah 17:7-8

[Most] blessed is the man who believes in, trusts in, and relies on the Lord, and whose hope and confidence the Lord is. For he shall be like a tree planted by the waters that spreads out its roots by the river; and it shall not see and fear when heat comes; but its leaf shall be green. It shall not be anxious and full of care in the year of drought, nor shall it cease yielding fruit.

Jeremiah 29:11

For I know the thoughts *and* plans that I have for you, says the Lord, thoughts *and* plans for welfare *and* peace and not for evil, to give you hope in your final outcome.

2 Timothy 3:16-17

Every Scripture is God-breathed (given by His inspiration) and profitable for instruction, for reproof and conviction of sin, for correction of error and discipline in obedience, [and] for training in righteousness (in holy living, in conformity to God's will in thought, purpose, and action), so that the man of God may be complete and proficient, well fitted and thoroughly equipped for every good work.

Proverbs 3:5-6

Lean on, trust in, and be confident in the Lord with all your heart and mind and do not rely on your own insight or understanding. In all your ways know, recognize, and acknowledge Him, and He will direct and make straight and plain your paths.

Proverbs 11:2-3

When swelling and pride come, then emptiness and shame come also, but with the humble (those who are lowly, who have been pruned or chiseled by trial, and renounce self) are skillful and godly Wisdom and soundness. The integrity of the upright shall guide them, but the willful contrariness and crookedness of the treacherous shall destroy them.

Proverbs 11:23

The desire of the [consistently] righteous brings only good, but the expectation of the wicked brings wrath.

Proverbs 11:27-28

He who diligently seeks good seeks [God's] favor, but he who searches after evil, it shall come upon him. He who leans on, trusts in, and is confident in his riches shall fall, but the [uncompromisingly] righteous shall flourish like a green bough.

Proverbs 16:3

Roll your works upon the Lord [commit and trust them wholly to Him; He will cause your thoughts to become agreeable to His will, and] so shall your plans be established and succeed.

Proverbs 16:32

He who is slow to anger is better than the mighty, he who rules his [own] spirit than he who takes a city.

Proverbs 30:5

Every word of God is tried and purified; He is a shield to those who trust and take refuge in Him.

Romans 6:12-13

Let not sin therefore rule as king in your mortal (short-lived, perishable) bodies, to make you yield to its cravings and be subject to its lusts and evil passions. Do not continue offering or yielding your bodily members [and faculties] to sin as instruments (tools) of wickedness. But offer and yield yourselves to God as though you have been raised from the dead to [perpetual] life, and your bodily members [and faculties] to God, presenting them as implements of righteousness.

Romans 12:1-2

I APPEAL to you therefore, brethren, and beg of you in view of [all] the mercies of God, to make a decisive dedication of your bodies [presenting all your members and faculties] as a living sacrifice, holy (devoted, consecrated) and well pleasing to God, which is your reasonable (rational, intelligent) service and spiritual worship. Do not be conformed to this world (this age), [fashioned after and adapted to its external, superficial customs], but be transformed (changed) by the [entire] renewal of your mind [by its new ideals and its new attitude], so that you may prove [for yourselves] what is the good and acceptable and perfect will of God, even the thing which is good and acceptable and perfect [in His sight for you].

Romans 13:8

Keep out of debt and owe no man anything, except to love one another; for he who loves his neighbor [who practices loving others] has fulfilled the Law [relating to one's fellowmen, meeting all its requirements].

Romans 13:10-12

Love does no wrong to one's neighbor [it never hurts anybody]. Therefore, love meets all the requirements and is the fulfilling of the Law. Besides this you know what [a critical] hour this is, how it is high time now for you to wake up out of your sleep (rouse to reality). For salvation (final deliverance) is nearer to us now than when we first believed (adhered to, trusted in, and relied on Christ, the Messiah). The night is far gone and the day is almost here. Let us then drop (fling away) the works and deeds of darkness and put on the [full] armor of light.

Romans 8:26-27

So too the [Holy] Spirit comes to our aid *and* bears us up in our weakness; for we do not know what prayer to offer *nor* how to offer it worthily as we ought, but the Spirit Himself goes to meet our supplication *and* pleads in our behalf with unspeakable yearnings *and* groanings too deep for utterance. And He Who searches the hearts of men knows what is in the mind of the [Holy]

Spirit [what His intent is], because the Spirit intercedes *and* pleads [before God] in behalf of the saints according to *and* in harmony with God's will.

1 Corinthians 4:20

For the kingdom of God consists of *and* is based on not talk but power (moral power and excellence of soul).

1 Corinthians 12:4-11

Now there are distinctive varieties *and* distributions of endowments (gifts, extraordinary powers distinguishing certain Christians, due to the power of divine grace operating in their souls by the Holy Spirit) and they vary, but the [Holy] Spirit remains the same. And there are distinctive varieties of service *and* ministration, but it is the same Lord [Who is served]. And there are distinctive varieties of operation [of working to accomplish things], but it is the same God Who inspires *and* energizes them all in all. But to each one is given the manifestation of the [Holy] Spirit [the evidence, the spiritual illumination of the Spirit] for good *and* profit. To one is given in *and* through the [Holy] Spirit [the power to speak] a message of wisdom, and to another [the power to express] a word of knowledge *and* understanding according to the same [Holy] Spirit; To another [wonder-working] faith by the same [Holy] Spirit, to another the extraordinary powers of healing by the one Spirit; To another the working of miracles, to another prophetic insight (the gift of interpreting the divine will and purpose); to another the ability to discern *and* distinguish between [the utterances of true] spirits [and false ones], to another various kinds of [unknown] tongues, to another the ability to interpret [such] tongues. All these [gifts, achievements, abilities] are inspired *and* brought to pass by one and the same [Holy] Spirit, Who apportions to each person individually [exactly] as He chooses.

Galatians 5:16

But I say, walk *and* live [habitually] in the [Holy] Spirit [responsive to *and* controlled *and* guided by the Spirit]; then you will certainly not gratify the cravings *and* desires of the flesh (of human nature without God).

Galatians 5:22-23

But the fruit of the [Holy] Spirit [the work which His presence within accomplishes] is love, joy (gladness), peace, patience (an even temper, forbearance), kindness, goodness (benevolence), faithfulness, Gentleness (meekness, humility), self-control (self-restraint, continence). Against such things there is no law [that can bring a charge].

Ephesians 1:19

And [so that you can know and understand] what is the immeasurable *and* unlimited *and* surpassing greatness of His power in *and* for us who believe, as demonstrated in the working of His mighty strength......

Ephesians 3:16

May He grant you out of the rich treasury of His glory to be strengthened and reinforced with mighty power in the inner man by the [Holy] Spirit [Himself indwelling your innermost being and personality].

Ephesians 3:20

Now to Him Who, by (in consequence of) the [action of His] power that is at work within us, is able to [carry out His purpose and] do superabundantly, far over and above all that we [dare] ask or think [infinitely beyond our highest prayers, desires, thoughts, hopes, or dreams]—

Ephesians 6:10

In conclusion, be strong in the Lord [be empowered through your union with Him]; draw your strength from Him [that strength which His boundless might provides].

Colossians 1:11

[We pray] that you may be invigorated and strengthened with all power according to the might of His glory, [to exercise] every kind of endurance and patience (perseverance and forbearance) with joy,

2 Timothy 2:1

So you, my son, be strong (strengthened inwardly) in the grace (spiritual blessing) that is [to be found only] in Christ Jesus.

John 16:33

I have told you these things, so that in Me you may have [perfect] peace and confidence. In the world you have tribulation and trials and distress and frustration; but be of good cheer [take courage; be confident, certain, undaunted]! For I have overcome the world. [I have deprived it of power to harm you and have conquered it for you.]

John 15:1-7

I am the True Vine, and My Father is the Vinedresser. Any branch in Me that does not bear fruit [that stops bearing] He cuts away (trims off, takes away); and He cleanses *and* repeatedly prunes every branch that continues to bear fruit, to make it bear more *and* richer *and* more excellent fruit. You are cleansed *and* pruned already, because of the word which I have given you [the teachings I have discussed with you]. Dwell in Me, and I will dwell in you. [Live in Me, and I will live in you.] Just as no branch can bear fruit of itself without abiding in (being vitally united to) the vine, neither can you bear fruit unless you abide in Me. I am the Vine; you are the branches. Whoever lives in Me and I in him bears much (abundant) fruit. However, apart from Me [cut off from vital union with Me] you can do nothing. If a person does not dwell in Me, he is thrown out like a [broken-off] branch, and withers; such branches are gathered up and thrown into the fire, and they are burned. If you live in Me [abide vitally united to Me] and My words remain in you *and* continue to live in your hearts, ask whatever you will, and it shall be done for you.

Hebrews 4:12

For the Word that God speaks is alive and full of power [making it active, operative, energizing, and effective]; it is sharper than any two-edged sword, penetrating to the dividing line of the breath of life (soul) and [the immortal] spirit, and of joints and marrow [of the deepest parts of our nature], exposing and sifting and analyzing and judging the very thoughts and purposes of the heart.

Hebrews 12:2

Looking away [from all that will distract] to Jesus, Who is the Leader and the Source of our faith [giving the first incentive for our belief] and is also it's Finisher [bringing it to maturity and perfection]. He, for the joy [of obtaining the prize] that was set before Him, endured the cross, despising and ignoring the shame, and is now seated at the right hand of the throne of God.

James 3:17

But the wisdom from above is first of all pure (undefiled); then it is peace-loving, courteous (considerate, gentle). [It is willing to] yield to reason, full of compassion and good fruits; it is wholehearted and straightforward, impartial and unfeigned (free from doubts, wavering, and insincerity).

James 4:7-8

So be subject to God. Resist the devil [stand firm against him], and he will flee from you. Come close to God and He will come close to you. [Recognize that you are] sinners, get your soiled hands clean; [realize that you have been disloyal] wavering individuals with divided interests, and purify your hearts [of your spiritual adultery].

James 1:5-8

If any of you lacks wisdom [to guide him through a decision or circumstance], he is to ask of [our benevolent] God, who gives to everyone generously and without rebuke or blame, and it will be given to him. But he must ask [for wisdom] in faith, without doubting [God's willingness to help], for the one who doubts is like a billowing surge of the sea that is blown about and tossed by the wind. For such a person ought not to think or expect that he will receive anything [at all] from the Lord, being a double-minded man, unstable and restless in all his ways [in everything he thinks, feels, or decides].

Zechariah 4:6

Then he said to me, This [addition of the bowl to the candlestick, causing it to yield a ceaseless supply of oil from the olive trees] is the word of the Lord to Zerubbabel, saying, Not by might, nor by power, but by My Spirit [of Whom the oil is a symbol], says the Lord of hosts.

ABOUT THE AUTHOR

Charlene Bolden, is a foster care alumnus who first entered the system as a 13-year- old in Tampa, Florida. At the age of 16, she transitioned to the Maryland foster care program when she relocated to Howard County. As a teenager, Charlene struggled to find the genuine support that she needed from the system while growing into an adult. Forced to navigate the uncharted terrain of living independently with no guidance, Charlene found herself afraid and unprepared for life on her own. But against all odds, she found an inner strength during her high school years. Continuing her own path to success, Charlene went on to study Public Relations at Prince Georges Community College. She received her BA in Communications, and an MBA from Southern New Hampshire University. Recognizing her gift for helping others succeed, she sought instruction from The Coach Training Academy, where she completed an International Coach Federation (ICF) and Certified Coaches Alliance (CCA) accredited, professional certified coaching program.

Charlene is a life empowerment coach who has shared her inspirational story with a variety organizations and individuals. She has spoken at independent living events and foster parent trainings to create awareness about the challenges faced by youth in the system. She is passionate about helping young people who are currently in foster care, as well as foster care alumni, to achieve breakthrough results that enable them to live fulfilling and joyful lives. Charlene is relentlessly focused on delivering tools and strategies that foster youth and alumni can use right now to improve their skillsets and business knowledge. Her personal exposure to the foster care system fuels a lifelong ambition to share her success with others, while instilling faith, support, and hope. Charlene loves to personally connect with those impacted by the work that she does.

Thank you for your support. It is my prayer that you end this book inspired, encouraged, and challenged to let go of negativity and to replace it with positivity. Understand that you have everything in you to live resiliently through every situation. I believe that God is about to move you forward by imparting the heart and mind of God. This is a time and season of surrender! Your surrender will be like a healing balm that brings liberty, joy, strength, courage, and peace. He desires to pour out His Spirit, release His favor, and open doors of opportunity in a way that you haven't walked in before. Allow this book to strengthen and prepare you for your next season. Continue to discern the times to know what God's will is for your life.

I am truly humbled to use my writing to share faith, hope and encouragement. I pray that this book ignites a fresh fire in your soul. With love and peace, Charlene Bolden

Website: launchingoutempowermentcoach.com

Twitter: @launching_out

40397152R00081

Made in the USA
Middletown, DE
11 February 2017